How To Books

SUCCESSFUL WRITING

WRITING REVIEWS

How to write about arts and leisure for pleasure and profit

Carole Baldock

D0528211

How To Books

Cartoons by Mike Flanagan

British Library Cataloguing in Publication Data
A catalogue record for this book is available from the British Library.

© Copyright 1996 by Carole Baldock.

First published in 1996 by How To Books Ltd, Plymbridge House,
Estover Road, Plymouth PL6 7PZ, United Kingdom. Tel: (01752) 202301.
Fax: (01752) 202331.

Note: The material contained in this book is set out in good faith for general
guidance and no liability can be accepted for loss or expense incurred as a
result of relying in particular circumstances on statements made in the book.
The laws and regulations are complex and liable to change, and readers
should check the current position with the relevant authorities before making
personal arrangements.

Produced for How To Books by Deer Park Productions.

Typeset by Concept Communications (Design & Print) Ltd, Crayford, Kent.
Printed and bound by Cromwell Press, Broughton Gifford, Melksham, Wiltshire.

Contents

List of Illustrations

Foreword

PLEASE DON'T BUY THIS BOOK!

I beg you. Spend your money on something else. How about some more lottery tickets? What about saving up for that dream kitchen? Or a few extra packets of cigarettes? You don't smoke – then why not take it up? Anything except buying a book that tells you how to write reviews!

I have to be honest. When I was asked to write this foreword, I thought 'Why should I?' It's like asking a seal cub to provide an Eskimo with a baseball bat. Why should I recommend a book which instructs people how to write reviews. Why help the enemy? It's almost as unbelievable as, say the British Government selling arms to the Iraqis before the Gulf War.

So why, as you can see, did I agree? Well, if you are still reading this vicious little handbook and are determined, due no doubt to some dreadful defect of character, to write reviews, then I'll tell you: if, as an actor, writer or producer, I have to get a bad review I might as well get a well written bad review.

Alright then, if you twisted my arm, and quite frankly if you're the kind of person who wants to write reviews then you probably go in for a bit of limb twisting too, then I would have to say that some of the best occasional writing since the war has been found in the columns of reviewers; in particular Kenneth Tynan on the theatre of the fifties and sixties, Clive James (*Observer* TV critic), Alan Coren (*Sunday Times* TV critic) and more recently Victor Lewis-Smith (*Evening Standard* TV critic). Naturally they all write with wit and, on occasion, bile. But they all know their stuff. They are knowledgeable observers of their landscape. They put in the leg work or, given the sedentary nature of the work, should I say bum work. They go to hundreds of plays a year or watch countless hours of television.

There is no doubt that if you want to do it properly, writing reviews is arduous work. It takes its toll. Most theatre critics are shambling individuals with that slightly bewildered look of a long-term high security prisoner on largactyl. And serve them right is what I say. Not that I'm bitter of course. No, I've forgotten all bad reviews. Especially that one in the *Evening Standard* of April 12th 1993 which said, when I was playing what

I thought was a really convincing bad guy in an Alan Bleasdale play at the National:-

> 'Jimmy Mulville's villain is as about as frightening as a Radio Two presenter'.

He was of course right; but how did he know I had based my character on Gloria Hunniford?

Be warned. Now and again you might actually like something. Extraordinary thought I know, but it might happen. You might rather approve of the soap opera from Carlton, or Sam Mendes' stage adaptation of the *Yellow Pages* or the new local French/Thai/Irish with the wunderkind psychotic chef. My advice when this happens is simple. Just say you like it. Yes, take that risk. Just state it plainly and clearly. I know it's more difficult to be witty when you praise. But, believe me, saying something nice now and again has one enormous benefit for the would-be reviewer. When you're nasty, the reader is more likely to believe you. I suppose what I am pleading for is balance.

Now you fall into one of two categories; either you are balanced, or you think you are. If it's the former then this is the book for you.

Whatever you decide, have fun and please don't send me your review of this foreword.

Jimmy Mulville

IS THIS YOU?

Author   Copywriter

                                        Playwright

Poet   Journalist

                                        Librarian

Editor   Designer

                                       Health writer

Researcher   Promotions manager

                                  Marketing executive

Publicity manager   Project co-ordinator

                        Head of community and education

Scheduling officer   Festival organiser

                                  Conference organiser

Press officer   Sales executive

                              National tour administrator

Advertiser   Events organiser

                                         Style editor

Schools liaison officer   Conference organiser

                                   Publicity assistant

Production manager   Secretary

                                    Editorial assistant

Features editor   Commentator

1
Writing Reviews for Fun and Money

It is quite easy to have a successful career as a writer, if you are prepared to work very hard. And provided you possess more patience than the proverbial saint. Reviewing makes an excellent foundation because it combines creative and journalistic writing. Yet it is often overlooked, perhaps because many freelancers assume that reviewing is either usually done in-house or commissioned. Also, the general attitude does seem to be on the lines of: "Those who can, **do**. Those who can't, **review**".

However, not all critics are frustrated performers or failed novelists, artists or chefs and they do provide an invaluable service. This book aims to provide a basic understanding of what is involved in reviewing.

This chapter examines:

- what reviewing is and who uses reviews
- the advantages and disadvantages of writing reviews
- how to investigate the market and explore your options
- how you can brush up your skills and learn more.

REVIEWING – WHAT EXACTLY IS IT?

Well, *Chamber's Dictionary* devotes a whole paragraph to it:

n. a looking back
retrospect
a reconsideration
a survey
a revision
a critical examination
a critique
a periodical with critiques of books, *etc*

v. to see, view or examine again
to look back on or over: to survey
to examine critically
to write a critique on
to revise.

THE ONLY magazine for people who need to be briefed about the arts outside L*nd*n

...the buzz...

Moorfield Lodge, GLOSSOP, Derbyshire SK13 9PP

01457 856492

Number 5   ISSN 1362-3931   April 1996

April is the cruellest month...

Death by 1,000 'standstills'

BRIAN BAKER on the barely hidden funding crisis

THE ARTS COUNCIL of England's 'success' in shielding artistic activity from the 2.8% cut in Government grant imposed on it this year by a once-off transfer of funds from the Lottery Distribution Board has led to the majority of arts organisations receiving a cash standstill settlement again. In Scotland and Wales, too, most companies and venues have been awarded cash standstill, more accurately described as a 3% cut in income.

Many will feel, particularly as the consultation period ends on Heritage Secretary Virginia Bottomley's proposals for limited broadening of eligible uses for lottery monies, that the arts sector is caught in a Treasury-controlled pincer.

If they urge that use of lottery funds for revenue spending be restrained, will the cuts in public funding continue anyway? If they back a switch in lottery spending will the Treasury insist the DNH axes support for the arts even more dramatically?

viduals to benefit directly from the lottery.

But there would be pitfalls and key questions have to be resolved. Who would select beneficiaries and on what criteria? It isn't as simple as helping Olympic Games hopefuls.

Manchester Cornerhouse director Virginia Tandy asks: "How do you get a regional spread and give young artists outside L*nd*n a fair chance of receiving money?"

Meanwhile, for many companies the cash standstill support is for the fourth year running. Administrators realise it cannot go on.

"We are getting to breaking point," says Yorkshire and Humberside Arts communications officer Sally Brown. "Arts organisations are constantly expected to produce more and more with less and less. It affects the quality of the work."

And, she asks, "Wh[...] authorities start to cut [...] too?" Already cutbac[...] support - which migh[...] inflation-proofed gr[...]

FLASHPOINTS

Hull Truck Theatre goes dark for three months

HULL TRUCK Theatre in Hull will close at the end of the current season in August and not re-open until the Christmas show in December. There will be job losses.

General manager Simon Stallworthy says: "The main problem is cutbacks in our grants and subsidies, combined with a changing market for our touring work."

Hull Truck has lost £31,000 with the demise of Humberside County Council.

Liverpool Everyman calls for fair funding

Liverpool Everyman Theatre has cancelled its summer season and staff face a four-month lay-off. The consortium of local authorities [...] at the

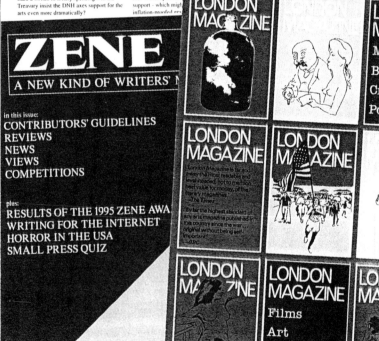

Fig. 1. Examples of small/independent press magazines, *Zene, London Magazine* and . . . *the buzz.* . .

BEGINNING AT THE BEGINNING

Reviews in news stand publications

Reviews come in all shapes and sizes – and styles; every publication is distinguished by its very own *je ne sais quoi*. If a single sentence, or the caption to a film still or book cover, contains some element of summing up, it is a form of review. So is an essay of several thousand words.

Most publications include a variety of reviews. For example, paperbacks, which may have earned a lengthy description the previous year when issued in hardback, often appear grouped together in a small section, each including comments of perhaps 100 words. Likewise videos, originally reviewed as films.

The latest book from a popular author or an expert in a particular field often inspires in-depth articles. These incorporate background information about the writer and refer to other books.

It's a vast market: if you buy a daily paper, plus one on Sunday and perhaps a monthly magazine or two, add up all the review items. Bear in mind, however, that a lot of in-house reviews consist of repeating or revamping press releases.

Reviews in small press/independent publications

For that first all-important step up the ladder, take a look at publications which often do welcome reviews: those on subscription. (See Figure 1 for some examples). Even the ones which don't include them may not refuse your offer; it isn't necessarily policy (*ie* lack of space) or the editor's pet hate. It could be as simple as nobody having thought about it or having the time to do it.

Payment is frequently minimal, possibly non-existent other than a complimentary copy. Nevertheless, many of these magazines have a good reputation; some of the main publishing houses and literary agents subscribe, keeping an eye open for good new writing. To find out more, see the further reading section at the end of this book or ask your local library for *The Writer's Handbook* or *The Writers' and Artists' Yearbook*.

MAKING THE MOST OF REVIEWING

Advantages

There are a number of advantages in writing reviews.

First

You get something for your efforts. There really is such a thing as a free lunch, and some editors will hastily point out that you've had a nice evening out, so what more do you want? However, one week covering a festival, for example, might otherwise cost you around £150.

The following are some of the ways in which you may receive 'payment in kind'.

- invitations to book launches; wine is served and occasionally a buffet
- invitations to private views of exhibitions in art galleries; again, with wine and a buffet
- press tickets to concerts (classical music) and gigs (popular music), with a complimentary programme
- press shows (film previews), often with coffee beforehand, drinks and sandwiches afterwards
- press nights at the theatre, including a free programme, plus a courtesy drink in the interval (sometimes accompanied by canapés or a buffet)
- restaurant meals and visits to tourist attractions
- books, videos and CDs
- merchandise such as clothing – T shirts seem to cover everything.

Marketing personnel tend to court reviewers, although being treated like royalty should not influence your unbiased opinion. However, you may as well make the most of it.

Second
Reviewing is a first-class opportunity to learn more about your favourite subjects. You could end up chatting to some of your heroes and heroines.

Third
It can do wonders for your own career. Networking is invaluable and reviewing helps you make a name for yourself.

Disadvantages
There are, however, a few disadvantages with writing reviews.

- You may have swapped a nine to five job for a seven to eleven one, with little time, inclination, or inspiration for doing any other writing.

- Some publications may prefer your reviews to your other writing – poetry or short stories, for example.

- There's no guarantee that even an urgent review won't be turned down at the very last minute.

- You must work to deadlines and to order.

- Reviewers are not always held in very high regard – especially where other writers are concerned (unless they want their latest work reviewing).

● You have to learn to prioritise and maintain a balance.

There are times also, when you can be faced with some tricky dilemmas which only you can solve. For example, suppose you have to write a restaurant review where the meal (admittedly free and undoubtedly abundant), was not as gobsmackingly delicious as the menu suggests. Do you comment, and upset the owner (never mind your editor) or say nothing? Suppose somebody goes there for a special anniversary dinner – on *your* recommendation? Well, as each case requires individual consideration, there are no rules laid down. **It's all up to you**.

CHECKING ON DEMAND

Ask your local library or bookshop for a copy of *Books in the Media* and you'll find three pages devoted to the week's most reviewed books in over a dozen newspapers. Books are the most popular reviews at 52 per cent and then videos at 29 per cent, according to one survey. Film reviews tend to get more coverage than videos, and theatre less, even though it encompasses plays, musicals, dance and comedy. Music in the media usually means popular and rock music rather than classical. Most publications include one art exhibition, and one restaurant. Tourist attractions usually come under travel.

What's on offer locally?
Even if you live in the back of beyond, there will be at least one, probably several, of the following:

● local radio stations
● community radio station
● local papers
● freesheets
● listings magazines
● newsletters (library, local drama group, art/film/music society, schools and colleges)
● student magazines

Student magazines sometimes accept outside contributions, apart from popular and rock music or film and video, which have people queuing up to describe them. In theory, students are too busy writing other things to become involved.

As for listings magazines, there are sometimes as many as five or six of them.

SPECIALISING OR DIVERSIFYING

What if writing reviews does appeal, but you have your doubts about being qualified? – I don't know much about it, but I know what I like and I really would like to know more?' **The first rule of writing is to write about what you know**. However, you can describe something you are learning about – it gives an original point of view.

There are more opportunities if you tackle a variety of areas, which makes **diversifying** a good start. Eventually you may need to reconsider and concentrate on your **specialities**. Curiosity is a useful attribute in a writer, but not when it means overworking to the same extent as the unfortunate feline.

Voicing criticism

Writing reviews should be done authoritatively. It is often thought the critic should remain impartial but many people enjoy reviews which sound as if the reviewer's chatting to a close friend.

With books, statistics show people are largely influenced by those on display, and by reviews. However, each suggested review needs to be considered on its merits. A book is a book is a book, that is, complete in itself. You may decide to ignore those which can be dismissed in one sentence, *à la* Dorothy Parker: life's too short; this book's too thick. Nonetheless, it is considerably harder writing good reviews than bad ones – people are always able to recall inspired invective sooner than they can a compliment.

Cinema and theatre may be considered fair game, especially the latter; each play contains so much potential. No two productions of the same drama are identical; it depends on the venue, the stage setting, the director, the cast, even the writer. Similarly, with music no two performances are the same; art always seems to rouse the strongest passions, whether for or against. If you do express your opinion forcibly, back it up with examples. But allow for other people's views to differ.

POLISHING YOUR SKILLS

Reviews aim to communicate, something which can be learned. A genius for writing is more the icing on the cake. It can also be a disadvantage – editing down to a particular length means you 'kill all your darlings!' Fortunately, *bon mots* need not be wasted; even the most purple prose will eventually match up with something. Writing is a craft which needs constant practice.

Selling yourself as well as your work

Some knowledge of marketing is essential, as is the ability to keep your self-confidence alive and well at all times. If you are wary of people you consider pushy, well, this is the way the world turns. Unless you are very sure of yourself, you will get left behind. Even in big business, employees go on courses in customer relations, not just to rid them of that unfortunate attitude: 'the customer is a right . . .', but to learn to deal with 'awkward' customers.

Low self-esteem can be overcome and confidence stands you in good stead in every area, not just writing. You can learn more about it from books on psychology and there are personal development courses available:

● assertiveness/confidence building
● how to discipline employees and correct performance problems (you never know, it may come in useful)
● speak confidently
● 'life was never meant to be a struggle'.

Lastly, you may want to learn more about your chosen area. A wide number of courses are on offer, some quite diverse:

● an introduction to looking
● popular music in the 1960s II: idealism and disillusionment
● the function of humour in society.

Going back to school
Further education and creative writing courses can be provided by:

● university, college, schools
● organisations – the Worker's Educational Association (WEA)
● writers' workshops.

Details can be found at the sites themselves, the Citizens' Advice Bureau and your local library. As a rule, they are widely advertised.

Doing it yourself
You can always teach yourself basic skills, or brush up on those you once possessed – see the Further Reading section.

Advantages
Some of the advantages of **doing it yourself** are as follows:

1. Courses can be expensive. There are usually copies of the books you require in the library or they will order them for you, which costs approximately 75 pence.

2. There may not be a course offering exactly what you want.

3.   It could be held at an inconvenient time.

4.   It may involve travelling quite a distance.

5.   You may not be eligible for a place.

6.   If you have children, there may not be crèche facilities.

Disadvantages
There are a number of disadvantages in teaching yourself basic skills.

1.   You won't have access to as many resources.

2.   It is sometimes difficult to keep yourself motivated without the discipline of a class.

3.   There is little opportunity for useful feedback.

4.   There are fewer opportunities for networking.

WRITING REVIEWS – WHAT'S INVOLVED?

Basic skills will give you the confidence to have a go at anything. What else do you need?

The first requirement is a desire to read and to learn. Read for enjoyment firstly, but thereafter be more analytical. Make the effort to look up new words and discover suitable synonyms. There's rarely room to embellish a short review with adjectives, so the one you select must be the most appropriate. At first, you may think: 'Damn! I've already used "outstanding"', but with practice, you soon come up with substitutes – without consulting a thesaurus all the time (at every opportunity, by the minute, constantly).

Interestingly, with the increasing popularity of anything to do with food and drink, there is now a specialist thesaurus because of the constraints of vocabulary. The first (and only) word many writers come up with is 'succulent'. Study a menu – you'll see it's a fairly limited field and very easy to get carried away with descriptions.

CASE STUDIES

Three entirely fictional characters have been asked to write for a new listings magazine. Dexter is to cover theatre, film and video, Brent will do art and music, while Katrina is in charge of books and the out-and-about section (restaurants, tourist attractions and so on). Any resemblance to living individuals is entirely coincidental.

Dexter Kavanagh is rethinking his acting career

Dexter is a mature student, now an actor (currently 'resting'). In fact, he has been resting so long, he's turning fallow, and despite a passion for theatre he's beginning to wonder if this is the right career. He is busy writing comedy material as his great ambition is to be a stand-up comedian. A very hard worker, apt to let himself get inundated, he needs to double-check everything and gets a bit carried away with bright ideas. Social skills are not his strong point; he really hates upsetting people.

Brent Bentley is out to succeed

Brent is a man destined for great things – and it's not just him who thinks so. An art student and lead singer in the band 'Qute', you could say he's a perfect stranger: tall, dark and handsome. He is determined to succeed. Apart from being extremely arrogant, he lacks empathy and always looks for the easy way out. He never bothers to ask for help or advice and is all out for number one, preferably that mega hit single. But the Turner Prize wouldn't come amiss.

Katrina Peters wants to use her degree

Katrina recently graduated with a BA Hons in English Literature and hasn't yet found a job. But the last three years have been fantastic and she really enjoyed herself.

Perhaps journalism will help her make the most of what she's learned? She hasn't quite got the hang of how to conform or toe the line, and as a perfectionist, she finds it difficult to compromise. She has some excellent ideas and works hard when inspired, though she sometimes lacks focus.

DISCUSSION POINTS

1. Does this kind of writing appeal to you?

2. Could you write for local publications, national publications, specialised publications?

3. What are your strongest points and your weak points? What might you do to improve the weak ones?

ASSIGNMENT

1. Review the local drama group's latest production, for a programme on local radio.

2. Review a book you have recently read, which you either loved or hated.

2
Making a Good Start

This chapter looks at working as a listings editor and examines the following:

- what listings are and what's involved in compiling them
- the advantages and disadvantages of working on listings
- how to classify the different categories
- how to make the most of networking through listings.

WORKING AS A LISTINGS EDITOR

Time Out recently advertised for an assistant theatre editor to 'cope one day per week with our comprehensive listings: a devotion to factual accuracy and a pleasant phone-manner are crucial'. The advertisement ends warning 'once a year panto fans need not apply'. What they don't warn you is that doing listings is not a particularly easy job. See Figure 2 for an example of theatre listings.

The aim is to get the right information to the right person at the right time, which, for a variety of reasons, is frequently beyond the capabilities of a lot of people. If you approach the editor of a local publication offering to help with listings, you'll be welcomed with open arms and probably a drink or two in the pub to celebrate.

COMPILING LISTINGS

Since the turnover rate in listings editors is pretty high, at least it's one job you stand a good chance of getting. Besides, remember all those tedious lectures you had to sit through at school or college? Wasn't it worth it in the end? Likewise, with compiling listings, think positive:

- It teaches you basic writing skills.

- It helps you with networking.

● It provides a primary source of market research.

The main reason many writers never succeed is because they can't comprehend what an editor's job entails. They never learn to get the hang of submitting work which is suitable for publication. Doing listings does give you some understanding of what is required.

Advantages and disadvantages of compiling listings

Advantages
A listings editor has to be organised, disciplined, flexible and able to work to deadlines. These are all essential writing skills. Another vital skill is editing. Faced with limited space and a lot of essential information, learning to match them up exactly is invaluable. Where space allows, you can start developing your own style. Make a start reviewing by briefly offering your own comments, *eg* another production of *Shirley Valentine*: 'welcome back to everybody's sweetheart'.

Disadvantages
Yes, you've noticed by now – boring. Listings have to be consistent so you find yourself typing up the same thing over and over again. The frustrating bit comes from convincing the publicity departments of various companies that if they need something promoting, they should keep you informed in plenty of time. It's amazing how many people think that all that's necessary for a bit of publicity is to ring you the day before. Then there are those who bombard you with details years before something actually happens. There again, if the magazine does not appear on time, and said event has past and gone, this does upset promoters.

Keeping people informed
One thing to remember as you tunnel through the paperwork is that a large percentage of people in your area remain oblivious to all the events on offer, unless it is something in which they have a particular interest. This is why doing reviews provides so many opportunities – there is so much competition to attract customers. Every art gallery, every concert, every book, every restaurant is battling against others of its kind to stay ahead. Those who own them will do almost anything to promote sales.

Everybody feels they are entitled to a large slice of the pie, and there never has been a pie big enough to go round – particularly where funding is concerned. The arts rely on networking and goodwill just to survive, never mind becoming an overnight (and everlasting) success. For one reason or another, everything tends to be hyped to death, so anyone's efforts to help are often richly rewarded.

THEATRE

Even if you are putting on a tiny production in a church hall, send us details.

BLUECOAT

School Lane, L1
708 9050

The Dark Perversity of Chameleons
FRI 9
Artaud's Blue Print in an extraordinary multi-media spectacle, exploring a strange world of mesmeric rituals, split personalities, surrealistic visions, sexual obsessions.
8.00pm. £4, £2.50 concs.

CHESTER GATEWAY

Hamilton Place, Chester.
0244 340392

Shirley Valentine
FRI 2 -SAT 24
Everybody's sweetheart is back again - Sunny Ormonde stars in Willy Russell's best loved play, directed by Sue Wilson.
7.45pm; 8.00pm Fri & Sat. Signed performance Thurs 15. £6.50; no concs.

Billy Roberts
MON 19
I see, another evening of clairvoyance.
7.45pm, £5.

CITADEL

Waterloo Street, St.Helens.WA10
70744 35463

Comedy Night with Frank Sidebottom
SAT 17
8.00pm. £4.50, £3.50 concs.

The India Rubber Zoom Lens
FRI 30
A Forkbeard Fantasy production, featuring the amazing, time-travelling adventures of the Brittonioni Brothers: "Brilliantly theatrical and very funny" (*The Scotsman*).
7.30pm. £4, £3 concs.

CROSBY CIVIC HALL

Crosby Road North, L22
928 1919

On the night - it'll be alright.
THURS 15 - SAT 17
A revue by the Dorians Drama Group, in their Autumn presentation.
7.30pm. £3.

The King and I
TUES 20 -SAT 24
Brought to you by Waterloo & Crosby Theatre Company.
7.30pm. From £3.50.

Welcome to my World
WED 21
Slide show presented by Jack Shepherd.
2.00pm. 30p.

EMPIRE

Lime Street, L1
709 1555

Sweet Lorraine
TUES 30 AUG - SAT 3 SEPT
Starring Mica Paris. Pre-West End musical spectacular from Clarke Peters, the author of *Five Guys Named Moe*.
7.30pm. £18.50 - £9. Concs.

The Life and Times of Gus Gascoigne - Trainspotter. The hit of the 1993 Edinburgh Festival transferred to the West End, and now it's on our doorstep. Worth investigating, & real live trainspotters get a discount.
Times and ticket prices as above.

The Crucible
TUES 27 - THURS 29
The Everyman Youth Theatre presents Arthur "Satanic" Miller's most renowned play, in a thrilling evening's entertainment.
8.00pm. £6 - £4, Concs £4 & £3.

FLORAL PAVILION

Virginia Road, New Brighton
639 4360

Old Tyme Music Hall
WED 7
Stan Stennet, plus full supporting show.
2.30pm & 7.00pm. £3.

NEPTUNE

Hanover Street, L1
709 7844

COMEDY CLUB
Steady Eddy
SAT 10
Australia's No. 1 Alternative Comedian, on his Quantum Limp tour. A cerebral palsy sufferer who "makes most other young comedians seem comically handicapped" (*Barry Humphries*)
8.00pm. £7 - £5.

Amigos
TUES 20 & WED 21
Cowley Drama presents a musical drama about holiday romance.
7.30pm. £3.50, £2.50 concs.

Lullabies of Broadway
THURS 22 & FRI 23
Featuring a young cast who are already veterans of West End hits such as *Miss Saigon*, *Les Miserables* and *Blood Brothers*.
7.30pm. £7 - £5.

Jane Eyre
THURS 27 - SAT 1 OCT
A new adaptation by Sue Lincoln; presented by Harlequin Theatre Company.
7.30pm. £7-£2.50 (proceeds to the Roy Castle appeal).

PALACE THEATRE

Oxford Street, Manchester M1
061 242 2503

Joseph and his Amazing Technicoloured Dreamcoat
UNTIL OCT 22
Starring Darren Day, this is something not to be missed, so I'm told.
Mon - Sat 7.30pm, Thur & Sat 2.30pm.
To book phone 061 242 2510.

PLAYHOUSE

Williamson Square, L1
709 8363 (7393: group bookings)

Only the Lonely
UNTIL SEPT 10
All your favourite Orbison numbers, with Larry Branson giving the performance of a lifetime. Your very, very last chance to see this show.before it's off to the West End.

FRI
A M
func
7.30
Ja
SAT
Flar
from
and
8.00
Da
FRI
A m
- joi
One
7.30

Ma
FRI
Tim
Mat
infa
Hov
7.30
PL
Tin
Ma
MO
7.30
EM
Thi
WE
Mac
of T
fi fr
is be
upw
10.3
Sat
sho

Out
THU
F'So
mus
mas
8.00
Fili
SAT
The
ers,
& p
betv
8.00
Thi
MO
The
awa
Hes
chic
8.00
A C
THR

Fig. 2. Sample page of theatre listings.

24

LOOKING AT THE VARIOUS LISTINGS

So how do you attract people's attention? That's something we'd all like to know. Many celebrities affectionately recall the time they were up at the Edinburgh Festival, performing to one man and his dog. Now every time they appear on stage, it's sold out.

One problem is the familiar 'can't-see-the-wood-for-the-trees' because of the amount of paperwork floating around: flyers, press releases, leaflets, brochures. The public are inundated and therefore sometimes pay little attention. Conversely, anything that does arouse your interest is the one thing which proves the most difficult to track down.

Listings usually cover the following areas:

- books
- art
- music
- theatre
- film and video
- food and drink
- out and about (leisure and travel).

Other categories depend on the readership, as will the order, which is frequently alphabetical. A family-oriented publication may also include events for children, sport, TV and video. Listings for young people and students will focus on clubs, fashion, music and perhaps film. Sometimes, usually for reasons of space, there's the occasional lumping together: clubs will end up under music (already jam-packed with classical, opera, jazz and blues, folk and roots, country, rock and pop), TV will be omitted and video added to the film section.

As you can see, there is enormous scope for writing reviews and, as listings editor, you have one huge advantage: you will be the first to know. This means you are first in the queue to offer your services and have a go at writing whatever takes your fancy. More importantly, this first step is definitely in the right direction since you are then in an excellent position to start offering your work to other publications. And you may even get paid.

STUDYING LOCAL LISTINGS

There is what you might call a technical side of listings, *ie* what information is required and how it is put together. Figuring this out stands you in good stead for writing articles and features which often incorporate an information panel to enable readers to find out more.

Where events are concerned, each section is usually arranged with the venues in alphabetical order, sometimes with the address and a contact phone number. The names will follow and then the date. The item ends by noting the times and ticket prices, plus venue details. Sometimes a brief description is culled from a press release or the wording is just repeated, spelling mistakes, over-excited ebullience and all (especially for fashion, clubs and pop music).

The duty of every press release, after all, is to convince the reader this is a 'once-in-lifetime', 'never-to-be-repeated' offer, and boy, will you kick yourself if you miss it. As editor or assistant editor or general dogsbody, you have only to make sure all the essential details are there, completely accurate and up to date. You can leave your readers to make up their own minds, unless there's room for a few kind words – or otherwise.

CLASSIFYING THE DIFFERENT CATEGORIES

Some listings are much easier to complete than others, either because they entail fewer details or because they do not change very often.

Listing the categories

Books
Books or literature depend upon your readership. This is usually the smallest section, and remains static as the details rarely change. It generally comprises the local writers' groups, invariably library based. Specialist bookshops might be included, plus those hosting events such as writers on tour. Poetry readings sometimes appear here, or else under the theatre section as performance poetry.

Art
Art is largely static, since many exhibitions are on for months. It can be quite an extensive section because displays are no longer limited to galleries and museums.

Music
Music changes monthly and as well as the various categories, is sometimes arranged in date order, then alphabetically, and either by venue or by the name of the band, quartet or whatever. This last seems the more appropriate since looking something up under the name of your favourite group is the logical way of going about it. Again, descriptions will be minimal.

Theatre
Theatre can frequently be the most onerous, not just because of regular

changes but because all sorts are included, *eg* festivals. The increasing crossings-over in arts and leisure, or interaction (if we really must call it that) between disciplines, can be confusing but it provides greater opportunities.

Film and video

Film and video is another section which changes regularly. Now that many arts centres show films, and the cinemas themselves are often multi-screen, some listings restrict themselves to the address and phone number. If films are listed at all, sometimes this is done as an actual review *ie* one 'film of the month' or a double-page spread, each item with a description of approximately 50 words.

Something similar may be done with videos, as a smaller section (perhaps half a dozen of the latest releases); they are rarely included in listings.

Food and drink

The food and drink section doesn't alter from month to month unless a restaurant closes down, opens up or changes the menu. Listings are minimal: address, phone number, opening times, perhaps mentioning a special offer or house delicacies, such as 'The Original Farmer's Arms': ostrich, kangaroo, bison or crocodile.

Leisure (out and about)

Leisure covers everything under the sun (especially if it doesn't seem to fit in elsewhere). Most people want to know what is going on in their area – and most organisers are pretty keen for them to find out. Listings include indoor and outdoor events, many organised by local clubs:

- lectures (how to wear a kimono?) and readings
- presentations and prize-givings
- stately homes and tourist attractions
- markets, fairs and festivals
- book sales, car-boot sales and jumble sales
- sporting events and horse-racing
- conservation, nature walks and gardening events.

Many of these can be written up as reviews, even interviews and features; they also come in handy for research.

Children's events expand listings considerably during school holidays: painting activities and all kinds of workshops, entertainments and visits to zoos or wildlife parks.

Arts **INFORMATION** *Digest*

NEWS & INFORMATION FROM NORTH WEST ARTS BOARD / NO 32 / APRIL 1996

Contents

This *Information Digest* is produced by the Information Unit at North West Arts Board. Whilst every care is taken in producing it, NWAB can accept no liability for any inaccuracies in it.

The next issue will be published on Friday 25th May; the deadline is Monday 13th April. Please let us have any material you would like included by then - whether by post, fax or e-mail. There is no charge for this service.

The *Digest* is mailed to NWAB's annually funded organisations, north-west local authority arts officers, other arts organisations and key partners. Individual copies are available from the NWAB offices in Manchester and Liverpool and can be picked up during normal office hours.

Our Manchester offices are at: Manchester House, 22 Bridge St, Manchester, M3 3AB; tel: 0161 834 6644; fax: 0161 834 6969. Our Liverpool offices are at: Graphic House, Duke Street, Liverpool, L1 4JR; tel: 0151 709 0671; fax: 0151 708 9034. Our e-mail address is: nwarts-info@mcr1.poptel.org.uk

North West Arts Board is one of the ten regional arts boards in England, which - together with the Arts Council of England, the British Film Institute and the Crafts Council - make up the national arts funding system.

The Arts Council of England is at 14 Great Peter Street, London SW1P 3NQ; tel: 0171 333 0100; fax: 0171 973 6590.

1. Opportunities

RSA ART FOR ARCHITECTURE AWARD SCHEME

The Arts for Architecture Award Scheme gives grants to encourage and enable architects, landscape designers, planners and engineers to work with artists at an early stage of a development.

Grants to support the artist's place in a design team range from £2,000 to £15,000.

The aim is to provide opportunities for exploration and collaboration, encouraging and supporting best practice in the field.

There are two types of award: INCENTIVE AWARDS encourage early collaboration between artists and architects in urban and landscape developments; PUBLICATION AWARDS encourage wider critical debate which focuses on the subject of collaboration between artists and architects working in the built environment.

Please note that grants cover artists' fees for collaborative work at an early design stage; they do not support implementation or other costs.

If you are involved or likely to be involved in a project which may benefit from this scheme, write for further details to: RSA, Art for Architecture, 8 John Adam Street, London WC2N 6EZ.

HAMLYN FOUNDATION INFORMATION (WITH APOLOGIES FROM NWAB)

The piece we included in the last *Digest* about funds for the arts from the Paul Hamlyn Foundation was, unfortunately, based on the regulations for 1995. We apologise to the Foundation and to anyone who approached it on the basis of the inaccurate information we published. The information that follows is based

on the 1996 regulations.

The Foundation is committed to a policy of making the arts accessible to the widest possible audiences. Because of its success the Foundation will now only consider support in places where successful projects have not already been undertaken.

Applicants should ensure that education and outreach work are an integral part of the projects for which they are applying, and that ticket prices or entrance fees are such that they will genuinely attract people for whom the arts will be a new experience.

Arts applications are under two headings: **Arts in Education** and **Support for Individual Artists**.

The former includes support for encouraging the arts in schools, after-school arts activity and collaboration between schools and other agencies to promote the arts.

A Foundation Award for individual artists was launched in 1993. Each year the Foundation concentrates on a new artform and a small number of major awards will be made.

The Foundation provides bursaries to selected institutions for students on a small number of courses which are outstanding in their field. No other student bursaries are given.

Further details from the Foundation at Sussex House, 12 Upper Mall, London W6 9TA; tel 0181 741 2812/2847; fax: 0181 741 2263.

FORWARD POETRY PRIZES 1996

Submissions for the Forward Poetry Prizes are invited from publishers, prize administrators and newspaper and magazine editors.

Now in their fifth year, the prizes are awarded in three

Fig. 3. Cover of a regional arts board newsletter: NWAB.

28

GETTING YOUR NAME KNOWN – NETWORKING

Listings are invaluable when it comes to networking; all you need do is ring up the press office (marketing, promotion, publicity) of the organisation concerned and ask for your details and those of the magazine to go on the mailing list. It's also useful to ask for a contact name in order to start building up a good relationship.

Thus, once you start writing reviews, and especially if you want to move on to articles and interviews and the like, you have a head start since you already know the people you will be dealing with. From being sent general information in brief, you go on to receiving press releases with specific details of one item at a time – frequently entreating you to do them a favour and give it some publicity.

Understanding the role of regional arts boards

The regional arts boards are an essential contact; they produce a regular newsletters which is sent to organisations on their mailing list. Figure 3 shows the cover of a North West Arts Board (NWAB) newsletter. As an individual, you can apply on behalf of the magazine or a local theatre group, music society and so on. Even if you're not eligible, there should be an outlet in the nearest city where you can pick up a copy. On average, it will contain details of the following:

- opportunities (including competitions and awards)
- courses/conferences and seminars
- news, including a lottery update
- publications
- jobs

If you do any other writing, performing or teaching, ask for an application form, so you can be included in their arts directory. All the arts boards have databases as well as web sites on the Internet so you may as well have your details as widely broadcast as possible. Incidentally, ignore any adverts offering to give you access to a potential audience of 38 million people worldwide – this will set you back about £100. The arts board will do exactly the same for you free of charge.

CASE STUDIES

Dexter can't face computers

Dexter learned about computers in university but that's now as much use as getting the hang of cave painting. It's taken him ages to word process the theatre section – one of them never supplies details in time and whenever he rings up, the press officer is 'on the other line' and never rings back.

However, it's all done except for this one item and so in desperation, he types in the box office number, and adds 'no further details as we go to Press'. Dexter wearily switches off with relief, but doesn't notice he's hit 'no' instead of 'yes' to 'save', so there's nothing down for this theatre at all.

Brent ends up with egg on his face

Brent types in press releases word for word in the listings; the design team can always edit them down – or out, as far as he is concerned. But the girl who reviews clubs doesn't mind doing his share, in return for a free ticket to '*Qute's*' next gig. There are a few freebies floating round the office but the editor insists review copies are handed over to be sold to help cover the overheads. Nobody agrees with this but Brent hangs on to his CDs, then sells them to the lads in the shops nearby. One night, drunk in the pub, they tell their mates about these bargain buys and the editor overhears.

Katrina saves face

Katrina tries to get free tickets for one of the biggest local attractions, the annual flower show, for a readers' offer. All the newspapers are doing this, but she is told their magazine is still too untested. She finally succeeds, but printing problems mean the magazine won't come out until after the flower show. Luckily, her aunt does charity work and the tickets are handed over to her office so the helpers can have a day out; a friend on one of the daily papers owes Katrina a favour so a photographer is despatched and the picture appears next day, with a caption highlighting the generosity of the flower show organisers.

DISCUSSION POINTS

1. How low is your boredom threshold? Will the advantage of working on listings outweigh the disadvantages?

2. Do you think in the long run that compiling listings will prove to have been a useful first step?

3. Will the opportunity to test out all the varieties of art and leisure help you if you decide to specialise?

ASSIGNMENT

List the weekly events for one subject, either film, music or theatre. Include a 50 word description for one item, recommending readers to be sure not to miss it.

3
Setting it All Up

This chapter covers the following points:

- the purpose of writing a review
- how to keep everybody happy
- how to equip yourself properly for the job
- how to organise yourself and your work
- how to introduce yourself to other publications.

REVIEWING FOR OTHER PUBLICATIONS

Once you've gained confidence and experience reviewing the various sections and you know you're serious about writing, you can start looking ahead and researching other markets. Perks and freebies are fine but making progress in your career and earning money is even better.

At this point, it may be a good idea to consider why it is that reviews are written.

The purpose of reviews

- to inform
- to promote or publicise
- to recommend
- to discourage.

In his article, 'Reaching a Critical Mass', published in *Acumen* (May 1996), John Marks points out that 'art and culture do matter to many, many people'. He quotes David Hume: 'Many men, when left to themselves, have but a faint and dubious perception of beauty, who yet are capable of relishing any fine stroke which is pointed out to them.' This illustrates beautifully the role of the critic.

At its simplest, a review passes on basic information. But it may also be written for commercial reasons, to help something succeed and make a profit. Occasionally, it could even be a matter of returning a favour.

The other main purpose is altruistic: supporting the arts in general and in particular books or plays etc.

Different views on reviewing

Perhaps you are promoting something to help a funding application for a theatre, even if the production is not particularly brilliant. Or, the event might be wonderful but the tickets are expensive. At its worst, you may be convinced that anyone coming along will be totally wasting their time. But reviewers are not omnipotent and there are plenty of examples of box office triumphing over soap box.

In the end, it is nothing more than one person's opinion, and everybody thinks differently. Not that you should mince your words if you truly believe something to be dreadful, but criticism should be as constructive as possible.

Reviews as promotion of the arts

Reviews promoting the arts are undertaken to encourage more people to take an interest. Interestingly, although first poetry, then comedy was claimed to be the new rock n' roll, the latest contender is theatre, following the success of the play *Trainspotting* (sorry, just heard – it's now philosophy). Culture vultures may swoop and insist the arts are in danger of descending to the depths but surely it is the other way round, offering more people the opportunity to reach the heights by discovering some of the good things in life?

At its very best, in the response conjured up, the arts answer the metaphysical need we all possess, even though some of us remain unaware of it and others never find the words to describe it. Such a need should be met by any of the arts, to help us understand, however dimly, that there is something to which we can aspire, which lifts us out of the mundane. The role of the reviewer therefore should be, in the main, to promote anything which can transport us.

LEARNING TO PLEASE EVERYBODY

Editors must feel stuck between a rock and hard place, keeping the customers happy *ie* the readers *and* the writers. Reviewers have to please the editor *and* the readers *and* all the companies they have dealings with. It's a balancing act, reorganising priorities according to each situation.

Reviewing is often considered to be a case of 'you let me have a ticket (book, video, whatever) and I'll write a review'. It's more complex than that, especially in the current climate where the arts struggle to survive and need every bit of help.

The relationship between reviewer and arts organisers, at best, is symbiotic. To put it inelegantly: 'You scratch my back and I'll scratch

yours.' Sometimes you feel other people have a somewhat different inter-
pretation: 'You scratch my back, and I, meanwhile, shall continue to
manicure my nails.' You may come across a surprising degree of apathy,
with a lack of organisation to match. People will claim to be so very busy
there just isn't the time to do any promotion or arrange publicity. It won't
be a problem for very long, not with that sort of attitude.

Getting reviews, good or bad

Worse still, as far as some people are concerned, whoever coined the phrase
'bums on seat' clearly had reviewers in mind. Ramsey Campbell, film critic and bestselling author, doesn't object to hostile reviews, providing
they're not 'ignorant' or 'uninformed'. He can't remember the worst ever
review of one of his books but racked his brains to come up with the best
one, on the lines of being recommended for 'people who think they don't
like horror writing.'

Sensibly, it's a case of '**no** reviews is bad news' and that's the worse case
scenario. In fact, the human race, having more than its fair share of
schadenfreude, will not necessarily be put off by a bad review. Sheer
curiosity may persuade them to see for themselves just how bad it can be.
One recent piece in a poetry magazine, discussing *Penguin Modern Poets
5,* called Tony Harrison 'incomparable' and Sean O'Brien 'exceptional'
and briefly concluded with the following sentence: 'And there is also
Simon Armitage'. This is uncalled for, being completely subjective and few
people would give credence to such a dismissive attitude. It is, however,
less damning than the conclusion to a recent book review: 'Give it to some-
one you don't like who can't read'.

Everybody is entitled to their own opinion, but where reviews are concerned, they can be taken very seriously. When taken personally, insults
and even fists, have been known to fly. Art critics have had petitions drawn
up in protest against them, and music journalists ended up locked in
lavatories.

EQUIPPING YOURSELF FOR THE JOB

Get up and go is what you need to be a reviewer but **you also need to be
properly prepared** for all eventualities:

- Make sure you have all the necessary equipment *ie* pen and paper, dictaphone – check batteries – and tapes. One famous actor, bored by an
interview, ripped out the cassette and broke it, saying: 'Let's start
again.' The interviewer didn't have a spare tape.

- Check you have a copy of the press pack.

Monday: Collect press pack from office. Check re photos – agent's phone no? *Must* read those forms and get them sent off.

Tuesday: Read pack and prepare questions for press call. And have a look at the new book!

Wednesday: Ring MC to remind YET AGAIN if cheque has not arrived.
Ring WF to check review arrived in time and when the next issue is due out.
Ring round for estimates to get computer fixed.

Thursday: Call into library – has that list of courses and info on funding turned up?

Friday: Rearrange interview – make sure plenty of time for private view afterwards.

Saturday: Tidy up diary; everything dealt with? What's coming up next week – double-check payments to date and expenses.

Sunday: Drop *everything* and get this piece of work finished and off to the publisher.

Fig. 4. An example of a wallchart/diary/calendar to help you organise your week.

- Carry your own directory of useful names and addresses.

- Make sure you have exact directions, including how you gain admittance to the building.

- Always carry change for the phone – and the number of the venue.

Clothing is something else which should be taken into account – not so much for making a grand entrance to the opera, although it is usual to don finery when visiting the theatre or classical concerts, posh restaurants or hotels – but to be comfortable enough to devote your entire attention to what is being reviewed. Cinemas are inclined to be chilly but art galleries, and sometimes theatres, are usually hot and stuffy. If you wear layers, these can be discarded one by one as necessary. Always choose sensible footwear – you can probably endure the most boring event providing your feet aren't killing you.

ORGANISING YOUR WORK

Taking notes

There is an art involved in taking notes and not just that of possessing a fair hand. Print, if necessary, and don't try to write about every single thing. Jot down **key words**, to help recall all the main points. Include page numbers when reviewing books; with performances, there's the programme to refer to. Any amendments or alterations should be legible and you need to be as accurate as possible *ie* double-check the spelling of names. **If in doubt, leave it out**.

Reviews invariably have to be fitted into a timescale; it's actually easier if you're working to deadlines because then you have no time to waste. If you are very organised, a wallchart or a calendar will keep you up-to-date by showing work waiting to be done and what's been completed. A weekly diary may be sufficient, but it's useful to have a calendar at hand to refer to. See Figure 4 for an example.

Ideally, reviews should be written as soon as possible, whilst the details are still clear. This is particularly important with book reviews because if you put them to one side and leave them for a while, you may end up having to read the whole thing all over again.

Similarly, it is a good idea to write reviews out in rough first rather than working straight onto the computer. Taking notes at the time can be distracting and you could miss something important. Learn to trust your memory; remember you have the programme, brochure, CD or book as an *aide memoire*. The end product may not closely resemble your first impression but even edited down, you can still manage to say much of what you planned.

Carole Baldock, 0123 456 7892
52 DORRELL PARK, HACKNEY BRIDGE, LONDON SE19 6XJ

BA Hons Librarianship and Information Technology.

FREELANCE WRITER: CV 1993-1996

Books:

Knight & Bishop Info. Packs: *Teenage Pregnancy: Bullying*
Cherrybite Publications: *Fiver Guides Writers' Directories*
Spike Small Press *(Partner; Marketing and Publicity)*

Book Projects:

Knight & Bishop: *Literature Guides for Schools* (ages 11-16)
Contributor to the Routledge *Encyclopaedia of Contemporary British Culture*

Editing:

Theatre Editor: *Merseyside Observer Guide*
Associate Editor: *Orbis*
Books Editor: *Event*

Regular Contributor:

(education, books, art, theatre, music, film, restaurants):
Monthly column in . . . *the buzz* . . .
Liverpool Star Series; Liverpool Post & Echo; Theatre; Writers' News; Freelance Market News, Writers' Guide (Fiction Focus series), *Quartos, Poetry Life*

Articles:

Assistant Librarian: Cap and gown . . . cap in hand
Library Management: Marketing the libraries
Ms London: Funny things – Women
The Scotsman: Single Minded (Mother's Day feature)
Manchester Evening News: Reading Volumes (book reviews)
Big Issue NW: Interview with Lily Savage

Other articles commissioned:

Art Monthly, YES, Young People Now, Dateline, The Good Companion to Britain, Discover Life Now, The Doctors' Post.

Book Reviews:

London Magazine, Writing Women, IRON, iota, Tears in the Fence, Zene.

Fig. 5. Example of a CV.

Finally, a copy of the published review should be passed on as a courtesy. Technically, this is the editor's or the sub-editor's job, but you'd be as well to do it yourself – then at least you're sure it has been sent.

INTRODUCING YOURSELF

Making a good impression
By now, you will have started to make a name for yourself as well as being on first name terms with everyone you have been dealing with: promoters, publicity officers, marketing departments, venues. If you plan on branching out, the next step is to start approaching the editors of other publications with a view to having your reviews appear elsewhere and getting paid.

First, you should decide whether to make the initial approach by letter or by phone.

Talking is good but is it better to write?
Both schools of thought are convinced theirs is the only suitable method. It probably depends on the circumstances. Sometimes it is better to make a brief call and follow it up with an explanatory letter. Sometimes you should send a brief letter then discuss the matter over the telephone. Some of us have an excellent telephone manner, others excel at the printed word. That is a more accurate deciding factor.

Covering letters
When writing a covering letter, remember the following:

● Keep it brief, relevant and always enclose an SAE.

● Include suitable details from your CV. See Figure 5.

● Make suggestions, but preferably not more than two or three. Where books are concerned, plan about three months ahead. Theatre – touring productions; art, music and film and video: cult section, anniversaries, something topical.

● Mention if photographs are available. They should be – more and more magazines refuse to consider anything which is not accompanied by illustrations.

Telephone calls
Make sure your telephone calls are:

● brief

CAROLE BALDOCK,
Freelance Writer

52 DORRELL PARK
LONDON SE19 6XJ
0123 456 7892

T.H.E. Editor
Bestever Magazine
Wonderful Publications
West End
London W5 7JJ

29th February 199X

Dear Mr Editor,

As theatre reviewer for the *Merseyside Observer Guide,* I've enjoyed reading your new magazine and am writing to enquire whether the following would be suitable for your readers?

What's cooking tonight, mother? About to tour nationally, this is the latest offering from up and coming playwright, Leslie Ferrett (it may be possible to arrange an interview). Set in postwar Britain, a family is torn apart by the sudden reappearance of hero Sid Bottomley's long lost sister.

Blue Swayed. A new musical, featuring talented Elvis lookalike, Elvira Henderson. The rise and fall of a major star as she attempts to conquer England; with 37 new songs.

Photographs for both of the above are available.

You may be interested to know also that my work has appeared in a variety of magazines: *Daily Splurge; Vivandi; Go For it!* and so on.

A sample of published writing is enclosed, together with a pre-paid envelope; I look forward to hearing from you.

Yours sincerely,

Fig. 6. Example of an introductory letter.

38

● relevant

● at a suitable time in the day.

Monday mornings tend to be frantically busy and Friday afternoons laid-back to the point of disinterest. Never ring the day a publication goes to press – apart from checking with the switchboard what day that is (and the name of the editor). Make a note of what you want to say; rehearse if necessary to give yourself confidence. You can learn how to overcome nervousness and gain self-confidence.

The advantage with phone calls is that you have an answer there and then. You also have more leeway to use your powers of persuasion since something could crop up in conversation which may not have occurred to you when writing. Or you can adjust your thinking on the spot, to match what the editor has in mind.

The main advantage of sending a letter is that it is positive proof that you can actually write. You can also enclose clippings of published work, which may tip the balance in your favour. See Figure 6 for an example of an introductory letter.

Approaching the editor

Approaching the editor should initially be done with great care and even greater patience. Editors rarely reply by return. If they do, it's invariably bad news – don't call us – ever! Figure 7 is an example of a rejection letter. Mind you, one budding writer turned a rejection letter to advantage, stating on their CV that their work 'had attracted the attention of Messrs Suchandsuch'. Cheating or creative? It all depends on your point of view.

Besides, unless you've come up with the best idea ever what will most likely happen is that it goes on file, the one marked 'could come in handy – one day'.

Editors get so swamped with mail they often take ages to reply; many writers clearly contact them under the illusion that theirs is the only letter they've had all month. It's not a good idea to telephone them in that frame of mind either.

However, once you have built up a good relationship and they know you can be relied upon to deliver good quality writing that fits the commission exactly and is bang on time, then they will start to contact you. Be good to your editors and you will find that they in turn do you a power of good.

CASE STUDIES

Dexter trips up

Dexter is asked to 'do breakfast with the ballet' although he doesn't know

Bestever Magazine. Wonderful Publications
West End. London. W5 7JJ: 0171 234 56789

29th August, 1996

C A Bladock
52 Dorrell Park
London SE19 6XJ

Dear *Ms Bladock*,

Thank you so very much for your letter and for giving us the opportunuty to consider your proposition. We do apologize for taking such a long time to reply, but I'm sure you appresiate we are always absolutely snowed under with contributions.

   We simply loved your ideas but due to circumstances completely beyond our control, unfortunatly can see no possible way of including them in the near future.

   We do so hope you won't be terribly disapointed and should like to bring to your attention our currant offer, saving you a whole 3% off a year's subscription if forwarded within the next seven days. You will also be automatically enter in our amazing Lucky Dip competition to win our 'looks as good as gold' jewllery set comprising: earrings, necklace, bracelet and rings, plus bonus gift of a cignet ring for the man in your life.

   Thank you so much for thinking of us.

Yours sincerly,

Fig. 7. Example of a rejection letter.

40

anything about it – 'Oh, you soon will!' the editor assures him. Well, there's always plenty of people eagerly firing questions so he can just listen carefully and make notes. Eleven does seem a bit late for breakfast, though. He should have been there at 9.30am and everybody else has left. Introduced to the prima ballerina, Dexter is so flustered he takes very few notes and then can't read them.

Brent falls down on communication

Brent starts delegating everything to an assistant who, overcome by being in close contact with such a star, is dumbstruck as well as starstruck. She can't bring herself to ask him to explain how to organise everything, nor admit she doesn't understand. Brent doesn't bother to help her out by issuing straightforward instructions and constantly changes his mind without making it clear why things are always being re-prioritised.

Katrina comes a cropper

Katrina hears about a new magazine and writes off suggesting a couple of book reviews. The editor, impressed, replies by return, then rings up before she's even answered; he offers her a double page spread as reviews editor. He really loves her ideas and sends a copy of the proposed cover for the launch issue – nearly every feature is one of hers. But Katrina has forgotten her usual motto: 'Enthusiasm is the most ruinous thing I know'. The magazine never comes out and the editor goes bankrupt, owing her hundreds of pounds.

DISCUSSION POINTS

1.   What areas of arts and leisure interest you most?

2.   What areas offer you the greatest potential for reviews?

3.   How do you plan to approach other publications?

ASSIGNMENT

Draw up your CV and use the relevant information in the introduction for a standard letter offering a review.

4
Reading and Writing:
Reviews and Literature

This chapter looks specifically at writing book reviews:

● the skills needed
● making writing your career
● learning more about literature
● and making contacts.

SETTLING DOWN TO REVIEWING

The following applies in general to all the reviews, but a book is a good example. You've read it – now what? That depends on the length of the review and your deadline. The danger of leaving it for ages before you tackle the review doesn't tend to occur with the other sections:

● **theatre** – usually submitted as soon as possible whilst the play is still on

● **exhibitions and films** vary, some being short-lived, others longer lasting

● **music events**, usually one night stands, can vary.

Unless you thrive on adrenalin and love to tackle huge piles of work in a very short time, do yourself a favour – make a habit of being organised. It can be hard forcing yourself to sit and write, but think of it as jotting down a few notes. Once you get going, it's quite easy to kid yourself along: 'Well, I've started, so I may as well finish it off now.'

People often ask: 'But how do you know what to write about?'. Put simply, it is the thing itself which inspires you (book, play, whatever). It's easiest when you can't wait to get your teeth into it, though that's sometimes more because you yearn to bury it rather than praise it.

SUMMARISING: THE BASICS OF REVIEWING

With non-fiction, you may not even have to read the whole book – last minute instructions as well as lack of space sometimes makes this expedient. Poetry can take a lot of analysing and so can children's books. The latter are often regarded as the most important, as they encourage the readers of tomorrow.

With fiction, first, enjoy the novel; second time, use summarising skills. These apply to all types of reviews:

- Pay very close attention.

- Understand what you're reviewing. Ask questions, if the need arises.

- Express yourself concisely, logically, clearly and fluently. Try to avoid making it read like a list.

- Watch your language, *ie* vocabulary; the intention is to communicate, not paralyse people with polysyllabic words.

- Your work should always be presentable, typed or word-processed (or on disk), including all appropriate details *ie*: book title, author, publisher, year, price.

- Keep in mind why you are writing the review and for whom.

- Back up your comments with examples.

The art of concentration

They say the art of conversation is dying, but concentration seems to be fading away in this 'sound-bite' era. For many people, reading a book has become a task. Yet even during everyday conversation, we may not recall every word and the advantage of reviewing a book is that it's at hand to refer to. With art, if you attend a private view, there'll be brochures available, perhaps a review copy of the catalogue.

Where music, film and theatre are concerned, you need to pay close attention, though you could make notes in the interval. Incidentally, any noise during a classical music concert, even as quiet as a pencil scratching its way across a notebook, will seriously annoy the rest of the audience.

Writing the initial draft

Don't worry about the length at first, unless you have an urgent deadline and must complete it as quickly as possible within the required word limit. With practice, you can usually gauge the right amount. Otherwise, try to include everything relevant from your notes, even if the end result is two or three times the length required. It rarely goes to waste, especially as this

Theatre reviews – main points

Theme:
What is the 'message' of the play?
How is it conveyed? Is it done successfully?
Is there a lot of inconsistency?
Do you need to tell the story?
Where does conflict arise? What are the points of tension?
Are other influences clearly visible?
Does it remind you strongly of another production?
Is it an old theme given a new angle? Does it work?
What makes it stand out from other plays (or not)?

Structure:
Is it a 'well-made' play?
Does it follow the standard: exposition; complication; resolution?
Is the plot so far-fetched as to be distracting or even ridiculous?
Any points of confusion?
Lost opportunities *ie* 'show and tell', a character appearing to inform
the audience about something important rather than it taking place
on stage.

Setting:
Is it appropriate for every scene?
Does it impede the action at all?
How does it add to the production? Detract?
What special effects? Do they work?
Have you seen it differently staged?

Characters:
Pick one word to sum up the main characters.
Minor characters – any scene-stealers *ie* worthy of comment?
How are the main traits illustrated?
Are they 'real people'?
Are the heroes heroic, the villains villainous?
Is the dialogue convincing?

Fig. 8. Points to consider when writing a theatre review.

initial attempt may come in useful later, as a feature or an interview. Figure 8 illustrates what may be considered when writing a theatre review.

The 'medium' version will be what was commissioned, while the smallest can join others in a round-up of reviews or a set on a similar theme. Before long, you will be able to edit down to the exact size in two or three attempts – let it 'rest' for a while before having one last go. It's surprising how often text containing not one dispensable word, can be sorted out 'just like that' a few hours later.

WRITING THE REVIEW

The basis of journalistic writing is a series of questions: **what, when, where, why** and **how**? With reviews, the first three are objective, because they deal with facts and form a framework to the whole piece. *Why* and *how* are subjective. Why did you enjoy this book, this concert or this play – or why not? How did it come to such an effect?

You may be called upon to sum it all up in as few as 50 words or you may be encouraged to go on for several pages. You may be asked to concentrate on the more positive aspects – because the company concerned has spent rather a lot on advertising. You may on the other hand, be ordered to be vituperative because the company concerned is now three months' overdue with its bills. Reviewing can be fun; it isn't necessarily always easy – like trying to juggle with a particularly sharp set of knives.

Planning size and structure

With luck, you will be left in peace to offer an informed opinion in approximately 200–500 words. Your first thought is likely to be: 'How on earth will I find enough to say about it?' Well, you very soon do.

Whatever area you are covering, there should be a little background information, a synopsis, plus your opinion, borne out by example. This should never be on the following lines, overheard when one film sub-editor was interviewing a wannabe reviewer: 'So, what is it exactly that you like about Kevin Costner?' 'Oh, he's *so* good-looking'.

The conclusion should be a recommendation, for, or, alas, maybe against. And don't give the game away. No matter how much you are impressed with the ending or the special effects, no spoiling the surprise for other people. For example, most magazine features have text boxes to make the layout more interesting and intrigue people with tantalising quotes. If one of these comes from the very end of the article, it ruins things for the reader. And if it was a particularly fine conclusion, it drives the writer mad.

MAKING WRITING YOUR CAREER

Reviewing books provides an excellent foundation for all kinds of writers;

it's the best way to learn and offers the most opportunity. Against that, you will find that where news stand publications are concerned, book reviews are invariably dealt with in-house. However, books still play an extremely valuable role in our society and inspire a considerable number of articles, features and interviews.

With a bit of luck (or some judicious timing), you could be successful by offering something based on the latest bestseller but with an unusual angle.

Starting small

There are other outlets where you might fancy your chances – and succeed:

- listings magazines
- student magazines
- small/independent press
- local press
- local and community radio.

Moving up

Book reviews are also useful since they bring you in contact with the main publishing houses. Of all the various organisations, publishers are usually the most helpful. For example, even if you ring the wrong one to remind them you have not received a certain book (hardly surprising, if they didn't actually publish it), you may find a bumper bundle on your doorstep, sent on spec in the hope that you'll help publicise some of their latest discoveries.

READING ALL ABOUT IT

If you want to start by polishing your writing skills, the best known publication is *Writing Magazine*, usually found on the news stands (if not, W. H. Smiths will order it for you, as with any magazine not actually on display). Details of this and other useful publications are in the further reading section. These magazines also provide market information, such as publications which include short stories and who may be interested in reviews of that particular genre. Newspapers like *The Telegraph* and *The Guardian* have writers reviewing other writers. Worth studying:- A. A. Gill (*Times*), Helen Dunmore (*The Independent*), Val Henessy (*Daily Mail*).

Ignorance is not bliss

There are plenty of books covering literature in every shape and form so if you want to find out more about literary criticism, are willing to learn and have a go, off you go to the library or bookshop. Theatre lovers, for example, can embark on a career as a critic equipped with little more than an in-depth knowledge of *Hamlet* and Sean O'Casey. And so what if you think the best definition of 'postmodern' is a 'useful expression for when you fail to come up with any other explanation'? You can still have a wonderful time discovering the classics, old and new.

If you don't fancy exams or even attending classes, you can take it literally and teach yourself. There are plenty of excellent books around about literary theory, covering every aspect of the arts (see the Further Reading section).

Going on courses

If the idea of studying at home alone doesn't appeal, you can always study literature elsewhere. Nearly every library in every town has a writer's group, circle or workshop or runs courses:

- writing for publication
- why the novel matters
- basic English grammar
- enjoying literature.

Publications such as *Writing News Monthly* include details of local workshops – see Figure 9.

MAKING CONTACT

The main publishing houses are based in London, each with several imprints who all have their own publicity department. It may be a better idea to ring – enquiry letters can end up passed from pillar to post and possibly disappear. The review copy will then be forwarded to the magazine office, but if the word 'shambles' springs to mind, you can suggest that it be sent direct to yourself. If you don't work full-time in the office and have to commute, it's more efficient, as you can start on the book straightaway.

Putting pen to paper

When contacting publishers initially, it does look more courteous, not to mention professional, if you write to them, providing you make it a very brief letter:

- Explain who you are.
- Tell them what the magazine is about.
- List which titles are required.
- Ask for your details to be added to the mailing list.
- Ask for a copy of their latest catalogue.

Creative Writing Workshops in Liverpool

Creative Writing Classes in Liverpool

Abercromby Writers Resource Group. Contact Jenny Roche on 0151 489 5274 for times & dates.

Childwall Writers (MAWW & FW-WCP) Childwall Library. Monday 1900-2100 hours Friday 1330-1530 hours. (Wheelchair access)

Homelink Writers' Workshop. Contact Michelle, Ruth, Sandra or Sylvia on 0151 498 4887 Tuesday 0930-1130 hours

Inklings Every Wed. 1300-1500 hours, Central Library, William Brown Street Tel. 0151 260 2241.

Kirkby Writers (MAWW & FW-WCP) Bette Martin. Phone 0151 546 3009 for times & dates

Queer Scribes - Liverpool-based lesbian, gay and bisexual writing group. Meets last Monday of each month. For further details phone Joe Lavelle on 0151 260 8990.

Liverpool Writers c/o M.T.U.C.U.R.C 24 Hardman St ,Liverpool L1 9AS. (Tel 0151 709 3995 for times & dates.)

126 Writers (MAWW) Contact Ms J.Martin on 0151 727 2550. Meets every Thursday (during term times) between 1330-1530 hours at Liverpool University Dept of Con.Ed. 126 Mount Pleasant, L'pool. 3.

Prescot & Whiston Writers (MAWW & FWWCP) Wednesday 1930-2130 hours at Prescot & Whiston CVS, 12 Aspinall Street, Prescot. Contact Michael Kirkland on 0151 426 0186.

Reaching Out Writers (MAWW & FWWCP) Friday 0930-1130 hours at Wellesbourne Adult Centre, Abborts Ford Road, Norris Green. Contact Sue McIntyre on 0151 226 3184 or Freda Renton on 0151 549 1541.

Roscoe Writers (MAWW) Wednesday 1030-1230 hours at Central Library (Roscoe Room, 5th Floor), William Brown Street (Wheelchair access).

Rose Lane Writers (MAWW & FWWCP) Wednesday 1900-2100 hours at Allerton Library.

Multiple Writers (MAWW) Thursday 1900-2100 hours c/o "Personal Services, Seel Street" Phone Mrs P. Carroll on 0151 707 0131.

Poetry Advice Desk - 1st Wednesday of every month 1730-1930 hours, Toxteth Library, Windsor Street, Liverpool 8. (Phone 0151 709 3688.

Wavertree Writers meets each Thursday @ 1700 Hrs, Harthill Youth Centre, Wellington Road, Wavertree. (Brian Francis)

Larkhill Branch Library, Queen's Drive Creative Writing Courses Wednesday 1400-1600 hours. Contact Freda Renton on 0151 549 1541.

Community College Courses

Old Swan College, Broadreen Road & Mabel Fletcher, Sandown Road.

Tues (CREATIVE WRITING COURSE) 1000-Noon

DROP-IN COURSES Mon/ Tues,Wed & Thurs 1000-1500 hours; Fri. 1000-1300 hours.

CREATIVE WRITING COURSE (Evening classes) Mon, Tues & Wed 1830-2030 hours

For details, phone Polly Barry or Maureen Peers at the Disk Centre 0151 228 0160

There are also CREATIVE WRITING COURSES at Colquitt Street and Myrle Street.

For further information, interested individuals can ring Student Service line on 0151 252 3106.

Walton Library, Evered Avenue.

CREATIVE WRITING COURSE run by course tutor Olive Carey For further details, ring 0151 524 1117

Fig. 9. Page from *Writing News Monthly* giving details of local workshops.

This also applies when contacting the smaller publishing houses, local publishers and those who specialise.

Exploring your options

If you are acting independently rather than reviewing the book editor's choice, should you approach the publisher first or obtain a firm commission to review said book from a publication? Both options can mean a long wait and not always a successful outcome. If the publicity department agrees to send the book (most of them usually do, once you explain the situation), at least you can read it and write the review whilst awaiting the editor's reply. It is very unlikely that you won't get it published somewhere. Even though small/independent press magazines have a very low circulation, it is a targeted audience and a review here is more likely to result in a response.

Receiving new titles

It can be difficult requesting anything other than new titles, *ie* something from the back list, perhaps for a themed section or one on reviewing cult titles. Some publishers have a policy of sending review copies of new books only; one company withdraws review copies two months after publication. This is another good reason for contacting the publisher in advance of being commissioned, especially as it may take time for their distributors to send a copy to you. Figure 10 is an example of a press release, publicising a new book. Where small presses are concerned, books are not remaindered quite so speedily; they are generally considered to have a shelf life of about two years.

ATTENDING BOOK LAUNCHES

Book launches take place in London, apart from local presses, obviously. The press release gives details, often offering an interview; press calls are comparatively rare. See Figure 11 for an example of a book launch invitation.

The author will give a reading, or appear in conversation with another author, or an interviewer – or a reviewer. More a public event than a 'sneak preview', it is intended to promote the book more widely and sell as many copies, autographed of course, there and then. Authors frequently go on tour to promote their latest book, giving readings in various venues such as bookstores and libraries, as part of a literary festival, or even in clubs, *à la* Irvine Welsh.

CASE STUDIES

The joke is on Dexter

Dexter attends a press call for an up-and-coming comedian but nobody else

Secker
&
Warburg

'Brave, vulnerable, intensely observant and articulate, packed with life. Ajay Close has made a splendid debut.'
John le Carré

OFFICIAL AND DOUBTFUL

A first novel by Ajay Close

YOU THINK NOBODY NOTICES. BUT THE JOKE'S ON YOU. SOMEBODY'S NOTICED, SOMEBODY'S BEEN WATCHING YOU A LONG TIME.

GUILT IS LIKE LOVE, IT EATS YOUR LIFE. NOTHING ELSE MATTERS. TAKE A LOOK AT THE FACES YOU PASS ON THE STREET. IT COULD BE ANYONE, ANYTIME. YOUR TURN NEXT. YOUR DAY OF RECKONING. HOW YOU PAY IS UP TO YOU.

All at once her mouth is open very wide. She is conscious of the attenuated strands of saliva between her lips, the salty runnel of tears; one cry, almost a yelp, and then it's over. It happens sometimes.
He asks to see it again, studies it, brushing an itch from his upper lip with his right thumb. Like the gesture boxers use in sparring.
'Are you sure it's for me?'

In a basement room of the Glasgow Post office Nan Megratta collects the illegible, the impossible, the damaged and defaced and delivers them to their rightful destinations. But when a blackmail letter crosses her desk, Nan finds her sequestered existence invaded by the secrets of strangers. The letter is intended for one only but from the barely legible address Nan Megratta identifies three potential recipients: a feminist legend turned newspaper agony aunt, a restaurant-owning entrepreneur with an unpalatable sideline, and a philandering Labour MP. Each is a public figure in the city, each believes he may be open to blackmail.

When Nan tries to discover which of them is right her ordered existence is sucked into a maelstrom of sex, politics, murder, and, most terrifying of all, disclosure. For Nan, too, has a secret; one she is determined no one will examine, least of all herself.

As Ajay Close's remarkably assured and compelling debut novel unfurls, the life that Nan has left behind intrudes on the present and the truth, observed through a kaleidoscope of intentions and emotions, becomes ever harder to distinguish.

Published by Secker & Warburg on 12 February 1996, price £10.00
For more information contact Kate Harbinson (0171-225-9383)
or Victoria Moore (0171-225-9353)

SECKER & WARBURG • MICHELIN HOUSE, 81 FULHAM ROAD, LONDON, SW3 6RB • FAX: 071 581 6243 • TEL: 071 581 9393

Fig. 10. Example of a press release publicising a new book.

HEADLAND PUBLICATIONS

38 York Avenue, West Kirby, Wirral, Merseyside. L48 3JF
Telephone: 051-625 9128

NATIONAL MUSEUMS & GALLERIES ON MERSEYSIDE
(The Walker Art Gallery)
and
HEADLAND PUBLICATIONS

Invite you and a guest
to celebrate

THE POET'S VIEW

Poems for Paintings
in the Walker Art Gallery

compiled & edited by

GLADYS MARY COLES

Wednesday, 15th May 1996
6. 30 - 8.15 pm

Readings and Wine

==

RSVP: to Headland, 38 York Avenue, West Kirby,
Wirral, Merseyside L48 3JF

I will be attending the celebration of *The Poet's View*
at the Walker Art Gallery on Wednesday, 15th May

(signature)..

and I will/will not be bringing one guest.

Fig. 11. An invitation to a book launch.

51

turns up, except the editor of a student magazine, who is a great fan. The comedian is even ruder to him than he is to Dexter. Having discovered that the editor of the local paper is also a fan, Dexter has his interview accepted for publication. Two weeks later, during a business meeting in the office, Brent informs him loudly that even though the interview was published (and the cheque was in the post), the editor told him that Dexter's copy was 'atrocious' and the whole thing had to be rewritten.

Brent gets involved in some funny business

Brent is very proud of one of his reviews and expands it into a feature, which is accepted by a well-known publication – on condition that he signs a contract saying it has not been published elsewhere. Well, a review and a feature are two completely different things, even if the contents are virtually identical. But copies of both have been sent to the band in a burst of unusual efficiency; their manager is a friend of the editor who issued the contract – 'Here's a coincidence' he says, showing him both copies.

Katrina could be laughing

Katrina has been trying for some time to have her book reviews published by a well-respected literary magazine. They like her work very much, but reviews are done in-house and there is neither the space or the budget for freelance contributions. She is then asked to review a book written by a member of the editorial board; once the author sees a copy of this rather glowing (but completely impartial) report, she changes her mind and asks Katrina for submissions. Six months later, another member leaves and Katrina is asked to take over as reviews editor.

DISCUSSION POINTS

1. What's the easiest way for you to learn basic skills?

2. Would you be able to face ploughing through books which seem to hold no interest for you?

3. Can you organise yourself sufficiently?

ASSIGNMENT

Put together a set of eight titles on a theme (health, hobbies) for children and adults, 100 words per entry.

5
Looking into Art

This chapter looks at the world of art:

- visiting exhibitions and private views
- ways of learning
- how to write up the review.

(AD)VENTURING INTO THE WORLD OF ART

Art reviewers often have a day job, trying to make a living as artists, or else studying the subject. This does not mean it is a closed shop, even if you personally loathe putting pencil, pen or paintbrush to paper. There's a lot to art nowadays and a more objective view can be refreshing, especially when the public at large entertains suspicions about modern art *ie* Emperor's new clothes syndrome.

Nobody likes to reveal their ignorance, so it seems much in art is accepted as given. Reviewers need to be very sure of their facts and aware of how easily they are setting themselves up in turn for criticism, should they express a view which goes against current acceptance.

Putting art on show

The larger exhibitions require more than one visit but almost anywhere these days can be used to display art. Even hospitals are often used as venues for exhibitions, on therapeutic grounds (visitors, as well as patients). Other sites (particularly during festivals or for special events) include:

- educational establishments
- ecclesiastical sites
- theatres
- heritage centres
- cafés and restaurants
- shops.

Some offices, such as estate agents, might fancy something hanging around to brighten up the place. Thus a review of a display set in the foyer of a company's office could be offered to artistic and business publications. It can also be expanded into a feature or an interview (with the artist, the owner, the organiser or the cleaning lady).

Understanding modern art

Modern art has a lot to answer for – trouble is, nobody seems to know what the question was in the first place. A lot of it is controversial simply because there is an element of fun – many people really don't like having their leg pulled. Furthermore, art is equated with paintings, perhaps sketches or sculpture, but it now describes a vast number of things: photography, print, mixed-media installations, video/computer generated imagery, *ie* incorporating elements from the other arts.

You may need to be an expert to be taken seriously when discussing Picasso's sky-blue pink period, but an amateur can do a good job with a more general review. Perhaps the important criterion in assessing a work of art is the one applied to poetry: you don't *have* to understand it. As long as it elicits some emotional response and you appreciate the concept, the work of genius (even if you haven't a clue what they're on about), that's a starting point. Art alone produces an instantaneous impact, good or bad.

Learning to focus on art

Reviewing works of art differs because there is not the same degree of study involved *ie* a film or a play must be watched, a book read, a piece of music listened to from beginning to end. Paintings or pieces of sculpture are not always considered in depth. Most visitors to an exhibition will have a look, read the little wall plaque, have another look, then wander off. They'd be hard put to give details, retaining only what they most enjoyed or disliked. Which is not to say that you don't find people taking a packed lunch to the Sistine Chapel, happily prepared to spend hours lying on their backs studying the ceiling.

If you like art, reviewing teaches you how to concentrate on what you are looking at and enjoy the experience to the full. And if this is your main purpose, well, why not? Being able to relax enables you to keep up the hard work.

Picturing art today

Where to start depends on how much you know and what exactly you want to know – it dates back a few thousand years, after all. You can go to exhibitions, then read up on what interests you or else visit galleries where your favourite works are on display. You can attend workshops or go on courses or join a painting class and have a go yourself.

A recent *Guardian* article had one of its reporters visiting three major exhibitions in 24 hours – in three different countries. He soon concluded that you certainly can have too much of a good thing; he appreciated Vermeer far more than Cezanne simply because there were fewer paintings on show and no crowds to contend with. And although it is good to see that the major art galleries in London draw huge crowds when they stage exhibitions or retrospectives, it is infuriating when you cannot get anywhere near the pictures for camera-toting tourists.

ATTENDING A PRIVATE VIEW

The world of art is big business these days, involving colossal sums of money and it can seem rather strange if you are involved simply as an amateur – in the true sense of the word. Reviewers and art critics are rarely held in high regard. Even artists who write reviews themselves often adopt a double standard *ie* whilst they are free to say exactly what they choose about the work of others, God help the unfortunate who demurred slightly when commenting on *their* masterpieces.

The term **private view** is something of a misnomer since it is sometimes a public gathering on a huge scale and people are so busy gossiping, and wheeling and dealing, that the pictures rarely get a look in. Everybody who is anybody will attend: representatives from leading newspapers and magazines, dealers, gallery owners, the artists themselves, plus friends and family. Figure 12 is an example of an invitation to a private view.

As regards the hospitality aspect, this can strike you as surprisingly stingy – no free lunch here, although the higher echelons may be invited to a post-view banquet. Food at a private view may consist of a couple of small dishes of crisps while the bar provides soft drinks and wine at around £1 per (small) glass. Since many exhibitions are sponsored by some very wealthy companies, you soon understand how they accumulated their money.

Having designs on you

By contrast, the invitations are extremely eye-catching, as you might expect; no expense spared here. The exhibition catalogue will be on display for consultation purposes but it is extremely expensive and beautifully produced. Press packs are not available, although should you require background information, some literature will be provided, usually in the form of photocopied notes.

A private view may last about an hour and a half and the best chance of having a look round is soon after arrival. Somebody is bound to give a speech during the proceedings, usually the curator, perhaps one of the artists involved or a VIP. This simply gives a brief idea of the purpose of the exhibition, plus the latest news about the gallery itself. The general

The DeVille Gallerie, Caratte Boulevard

is delighted to invite YOU
to the opening of their latest
spectacular exhibition:

John Q. Smith: 87 years an artist

A never-before-seen collection of every
one of his major works.

Preview: 6.30pm until 7.30pm;
thereafter, to adjourn to:

The Bar Barbara Anne, 71 Quilt Street.

BRING THIS INVITE AND GET 50% OFF
A CARAFE OF HOUSE WINE!!!

The DeVille Gallerie would like to thank all its sponsors
for making this exhibition possible.

Fig. 12. Invitation to a private view.

With Compliments
Carole Baldock Freelance Writer
52 Dorrell Park, London SE19 6XJ.
0123 456 7892

Carole Baldock, Freelance Writer
52 Dorrell Park, London SE19 6XJ. 0123 456 7892
With Compliments

Carole Baldock, Freelance Writer
52 Dorrell Park, London SE19 6XJ. 0123 456 7892

With Compliments

CAROLE BALDOCK, FREELANCE WRITER: 0123 456 7892
51 DORRELL PARK, HACKNEY BRIDGE, LONDON E9 6XJ

CAROLE BALDOCK, FREELANCE WRITER
0123 456 7892
51 DORRELL PARK, HACKNEY BRIDGE, LONDON E9 6XJ

CAROLE BALDOCK
FREELANCE WRITER

52 Dorrell Park
London SE19 6XJ
0123 456 7892

CAROLE BALDOCK
Freelance Writer

52 Dorrell Park
London SE19 6XJ
0123 456 7892

Fig. 13. Examples of letterheads and compliments slips.

sequence of events is usually as follows: three-quarters of an hour circulating, fifteen minutes speech, roughly half an hour to carry on chatting or actually wander around the exhibition.

STUDYING ART

Reading up: magazines and books

Some publications are of practical interest, others, such as *The Burlington Magazine* and *London Magazine* concentrate on the history of art. There are many excellent and extremely beautiful books on the subject (see the Further Reading section). All the Sunday supplements include art reviews, with occasional articles – usually when Damien Hirst or Rachel Whiteread has won yet another prize.

Courses on art

Invariably aimed at those who wish to practise, there are some for students who want to understand more and thus deepen their appreciation. Art, like many other disciplines which form part of the humanities, overlaps into media, cultural studies and so on; screen studies might relate to film (silver) or printing (silk), just as visual studies could be art, film or video.

Putting art into practice

If you're considering a career in freelance writing, practical experience in graphic design and photography could prove useful. Marketing yourself starts with creating a good first impression and you can easily do this if you devise a classy letterhead and compliments slip. See Figure 13.

You also improve your chances (doubling them, allegedly) if you offer your own photographs to accompany articles, features and interviews. Even if you are more interested in art as a hobby, these are some of the classes available:

- visual approach to character (relating text to painting, photography and drawn images)
- nineteenth-century British art
- the role of museums and the arts in urban renewal
- calligraphy and lettering

LEARNING MORE

Gallery facilities

Many courses, workshops and day-schools at colleges and universities are arranged in conjunction with current exhibitions to enable people to make the most of the experience. Most galleries and arts centres organise a series of talks, frequently free, which enable the public (and, of course, you, the reviewer) to find out more about the works on show and the artists themselves. They may also hold forums or debates:

- Fine arts versus installations.

- Will art now make the same impact in a hundred years' time, as nine-teenth-century art does today?

Art in education and the community

Many venues have an education secretary who devises programmes, involving both theory and practice, to interest children, adults and the community in general. For example, discussing the gallery's policy towards acquiring new works. Lectures are given by authors, curators, artists and, like the guided tours, are often free. The latter last for about half an hour but you can find out more from the information assistants who also give introductory talks to groups.

It is not as easy to get involved with galleries in the same way as theatre or music, although there are organisations you can join. For the friends of Liverpool's Tate Gallery for example, this means a variety of benefits:

- invitations to private views and special events
- a copy of *tate: The art magazine*
- bookshop discounts.

Art fairs

Some artists are inclined to be disdainful about these events – unless they have been invited to submit work. Usually, so much is on offer, there's enough to keep everybody happy. London dealers set up shop with their finest wares on display; museums provide computers for you to 'browse' through their collections and there is often a series of interesting lectures, delivered by eminent names.

WRITING THE REVIEW

Not all reviews incorporate illustrations or photographs, especially as there is rarely the space. However, editors like to make use of them where possible as too much text is seen as being 'reader-unfriendly'. An art review without pictures is rather pointless. Figure 14 is an extract from . . . *the buzz* . . .

Reviews of exhibitions will be dealt with in-depth by those involved in the art world. The amateur can still include a certain amount of background information about the artist, some, if available, about influences and the

more

Scenes

from provincial life

IT WAS very heartening to find so many people visiting the Liverpool Tate, not on a rainy lunchtime but one of the first bright days of spring. Rather more having a look at the Young Tate exhibition *Testing The Water* than *Home and Away: Internationalism and British Art* but both were exceptionally good. The latter (reviewed in ...the buzz.. number 3) is a vibrant mixture of painting, sculpture and installations, both fascinating and poignant (teacher to class, sitting around Dod Proctor's delicate portrait, *Morning*: "Just as we have here a young girl about to wake up, could we perhaps say that she is at the dawn of womanhood? Or am I perhaps reading too much into it?")

As for art for art's sake, I must say that when it comes to Rachel Whiteread's *Untitled (Airbed II)*, for all the big words in the text (Life, Death, you know the ones), a mattress propped against a wall has more to do with furniture removal than art. I think maybe it's the title which is more annoying than anything. And Damien Hirst's 1991 *Forms Without Life*, which appears to be a display cabinet knocked up by MFI, filled with huge, gloriously shaped and coloured shells from Thailand, does have a certain *je ne sais quoi*. Or rather, I think I do know - Sunday supplement undertones. Never mind, there was plenty of consolation, plenty to uplift the soul - Hockney, Gwen John, Barbara Hepworth and Stanley Spencer.

New Contemporaries 96, April 13 - May 27; Young Tate workshops, second Sunday each month, 11.00am-4.00pm; The Great Art Adventure (family programme), third weekend each month, 1.30-4.30pm. All free. Details 0151 709 3223.

Fig. 14. An art review in . . . *the buzz* . . .

genesis of the piece. Thereafter, the review would concentrate on how they personally reacted to an exhibition, though in this area, opinions should perhaps be advanced rather more cautiously than in any other of the arts.

CASE STUDIES

Dexter creates the wrong impression

Dexter is not keen on art, but he is keen on doing Brent a favour, visiting a new exhibition on his behalf. Chatting to the magazine's art editor, who is something of a celebrity, and hoping to get into his good books, Dexter casually mentions that he knows one of the most influential critics, whom he has just spotted. The art editor sets off in hot pursuit, the said critic having been absolutely savage about his last exhibition. Dexter departs, having noticed with alarm that the art editor has finished his bottle of beer but still has an ominously firm grip around the neck.

Brent's artistic licence

Brent is talked into doing a series on the arts courses available throughout the city, none of which he enjoys except graphic design. He decides it's about time 'Qute' got their act together and comes up with ideas for T shirts, album covers, posters and flyers. Forgetting the notorious reputation of printers, who are always blamed for magazines (and not just theirs) forever running out of money and coming out late, he insists he cannot settle for less than the best and ignores the fact that all the estimates amount to the whole of the band's budget.

Katrina thinks she's sitting pretty

Katrina's favourite treat is art books and she has learned a considerable amount from them. But it's an expensive interest, or has been up until now when she can order review copies. Then the editor insists she reviews something completely different, like books on sport. She decides to contact other publications and offer them some reviews. Unfortunately, she doesn't get round to reading the Sunday supplement which is the first one she writes to, or she'd have known that they don't include reviews of art or any other books.

DISCUSSION POINTS

1. Art now covers so many different areas. How will you decide whether any of them is right for you?

2. Are there advantages in utilising some of what you have learned and putting your new skills into practice – in design, for example?

3.   Do you now find yourself automatically making more of a critical assessment rather than just reading magazines, looking at posters and so on?

ASSIGNMENT

Design a flyer promoting a company whose work you don't much care for, to submit to a company with whom you would really like to work.

How to Write for Television
William Smethurst

Television is a huge and expanding market for the freelance writer. Particularly in the field of drama, producers are constantly looking for new writers for situation comedies, series drama, and soap operas and single plays. But what kind of scripts are required? How should a script be presented and laid out? What camera moves should you put in, and should you plan for commercial breaks? Packed with hard-hitting information and advice, and illustrated throughout with examples, this is a complete step-by-step manual for every writer wanting to break into this lucrative market. 'Invest in a copy.' *BAFTA News.* 'Your best starting point.' *Writers News.*

£8.99, 160 pp illus. 1 85703 045 1

Please add postage & packing (UK £1 per copy,
Europe £2 per copy, World £3 per copy airmail).

How To Books Ltd, Plymbridge House, Estover Road,
Plymouth PL6 7PZ, United Kingdom.
Tel: (01752) 202301. Fax: (01752) 202331.

Credit card orders may be faxed or phoned.

6
Listening out for Music

This chapter concentrates on writing music reviews:

- the various categories of music and their appeal
- contacting record companies
- collecting local information and attending a press launch
- writing the review
- reviewing for local radio

TALKING ABOUT TODAY'S MUSIC

Everybody loves music of one kind or another, often to the point of chauvinism: the highbrow looks down upon the lowbrow and everybody despises 'heavy metal' fans. As with art, you don't have to do it yourself to be able to appreciate it. Many people do have a nodding acquaintance with a musical instrument in some shape or form – guitars spring to mind, or the ubiquitous school recorders.

Music has many categories: classical, opera, operetta, easy listening, middle of the road, folk, country and western, jazz, blues, world music plus all the interpretations of 'popular music', which naturally includes rock n' roll. Reviews fall into two main categories:

- very easy listening, in the comfort of your own armchair at home (*ie* CDs, cassettes and vinyl)
- going out to concerts and gigs.

Musical chairs – the old and the new

Reviews are mostly of the easy listening kind and albums rather than singles, unless you are writing for a daily or a weekly publication, since concerts and gigs are invariably one night stands. Where touring productions of musicals and opera are concerned, reviews are used, although, with both classical and popular music, features, interviews and previews are usually required.

Reviewing concerts and gigs is a little easier for the novice than

MORE MUSIC

Headbanger's Bawl

THE following is a severe guide as to what's completely chronic, and another album that isn't bad.

Firstly, THE LEVELLERS' latest platter, 'ZEITGEIST' (why isn't that title intriguing?), can easily be described in one word, but I'll use three instead. Dull, dull, dull. It's like' some dreadful alternative rock crap that just won't die, e.g. latest single 'HOPE(less) ST.'; if you buy this, I'll find out where you live, go round and hit you several times with mouldy old fiddle. Do yourself a favour and buy a Manic Street Preachers album instead.

WORMHOLE were inspired by Bart Simpson for their title 'CHICKS DIG SCARS'. The 'music' on this debut effort is sinister, and slower than a snail on sedatives, like the Cranberries gone gothic. The vocals are whispered and whined, - and the current 3-chord trend is used excessively - between three songs, with a chord each. In fact, it's a very boring album nearly as tragic as Oasis.

While the music isn't so bad, BUCKSHOT O.D.'s 'OUTTA COARSE' is completely laughable. You can't take seriously a band with such ludicrous titles: 'Buss Dem Caps', 'Pigsty Le', and the atrocious 'Smelly Belly Up'; forgive me for being prejudiced against the terminally stupid, but they really shouldn't have printed the lyrics. Granted, they've taken the essence of the hardcore gangster rap/metal hybrid, but ended up creating a parody with the presentation. And the singer,

whilst trying to sound like Ice T, ends up with the integrity of Snow or Shaggy.

CIV, however, is instantly lovable, as 'SET YOUR GOALS's opening sounds like the intro to the Ren and Stimpy show, and each song laced with the sensibilities of a potential punk/pop label. Anyhow, after the fourth or fifth listen, the hardcore hooks'l grab you, especially 'Can't Wait One Minute More'. And on the subject of naming the band after himself, singer Civ says, "Pretentious? Moi?"

Quote of the day is The Flaming Lips vocalist/ guitarist Wayne 'Wacky Git' Coyne: 'I love anarchy in music...Anarchy in everyday life, though, wouldn't be so

cool. Anarchy at the grocery store would suck, because you'd go to buy a can of beans and there'd be tuna fish or something in it!"

I leave you on a happy note, as news has swung my way that the Manics have been practising together recently, and a London gig is imminent. And if anybody starts whinging on about how unfair the band is being to Richey, I'll send the Levellers round to their abode to play extended fiddle solos.

CASSIA,

Fig. 15. Music review from *The Guide*.

reviewing CDs; the latter demands specialised knowledge. With the former, you will be describing the surroundings, the atmosphere and so forth; at least one leading reviewer tends to include a single paragraph about a specific album out of the whole of a regular column.

But is classical music best left to the experts? It can be difficult to have reviews accepted by other publications unless you are something of a specialist. Nor are you likely to receive much payment. This is the sphere of dedicated amateurs and famous professionals. Fortunately, the world of classical music, like that of ballet and the opera, is keen to entice the man (and woman and child) in the street. That's where you come in.

Conversely, popular music is one of the easiest fields to break into. So much hype surrounds the music industry that every promoter and record company make huge efforts to get artistes noticed. With the colossal demand for reviews and interviews, you can even have 16-year-olds writing their own column for the local listings magazine (see Figure 15).

CONTACTING RECORD COMPANIES

It can be tricky to get your foot in the door because this industry, again, is **big** business. Reviews are generally seen as being for commercial purposes, *ie* to assist said companies to make even more profit.

Record shops have on-line information, listing everything anyone ever needed to know about the music industry (record labels, recording studios, the lot). This is also available in directories *(Musicmaster, Teletunes, Musicweek)* and your music sub-editor should have a copy. Since they can be rather expensive *(Musicmaster* is huge and costs about £90), if they don't, you will either have to borrow it from your mate behind the counter or go down to the local bookstore and browse, pen and pad in hand.

Mailing lists and marketing

To get on the mailing lists requires a fax or letter of confirmation from the editor, a copy of the magazine and perhaps some cuttings of published work. Most marketing departments in record companies will be happy to provide review copies, even if you are writing for a fanzine. What counts is that it is a targeted audience *ie* one dedicated to a certain kind of music, a particular band, and therefore, far more likely to respond.

Glossy magazines may have a huge circulation but not all the readers will be so fascinated by just one of the subjects covered that they bother to react. Some editors of student magazines claim they are not taken seriously – it is hardly sensible to ignore the potential of a huge market, especially considering many student writers could be tomorrow's bestselling authors.

The best things in life are free

Once on the mailing list, you are sent press releases detailing upcoming tours, special appearances and newly released CDs. Having established a good relationship, you usually find that record companies are very helpful. Along with review copies of CDs, they can provide competition prizes or readers' offers, and other merchandise: posters, novelty items like key rings, T shirts or sweatshirts.

They will send free tickets for **gigs**, arrange telephone or live interviews and have been known to make long distance calls to check you are available and assure you that the interview will go really well. They may offer to pay for the taxi fare or to arrange for your favourite guitarist to ring up for a chat – so that's how to be the envy of all your friends. A word of advice, though, no matter how proud you are of your nice, new (free) sweatshirt, don't wear it if you're interviewing another band.

Nobody is quite sure how the word **ligging** originated *ie* getting everything for nothing, but everybody tends to associate it with the music industry.

READING UP AND FINDING OUT MORE

Bear in mind that the word **classic** is often applied to the likes of recording artistes such as Phil Collins. However, even the heavyweight newspapers seem to give equal billing to classical and popular music, whether it be an entire page or just one column. Tully Potter has some entertaining comments on the former, likewise Chrissy Illey on the latter. Tom Hibbert in the *Mail on Sunday* and most of the writers in *The Daily Telegraph* are well worth perusing.

There is a huge range of music magazines covering popular music; classical fans are catered for by the likes of *Classic FM* and *Classic CD*. Useful books are listed in the further reading section, including the Usborne guide *Understanding Music,* for those of you who still don't know your Mozart from your Elgar.

Finding out about courses

Short of joining a choir, a folk group or a band, there are not many opportunities to approach music in a practical manner, since courses, though wide-ranging, cater for those who fancy music as a hobby. They cover rather esoteric aspects, though some of them should prove handy:

* introduction to music journalism
* studying popular music
* singing for fun and confidence
* music for pleasure (*ie* listening, not playing).

Courses in colleges take it more seriously. A light music college diploma provides training which ranges from the performing side (including improvisation) to the more academic *ie* musicianship and theory. Music often forms part of a creative arts course.

Music in the community is catered for in other venues, such as theatres: big bands, youth orchestras, lunch-time concerts, jazz workshops, small scale music festivals.

GETTING TO KNOW WHAT'S ON LOCALLY

Even classical music is no longer confined to the imposing concert hall or town hall, cathedral or theatre. Patrons of café bars and restaurants are entertained by string quartets, displays in galleries, arts centres or museums enhanced by live performances. Nearly every pub, bar and club likewise seeks to keep its customers happy with special nights featuring: singers, Latin, jazz, blues, R n' B, folk, country, in fact everything from karaoke to Ceilidhs. All or any of these can be reviewed.

Looking at carnival time

Now more commonly known as festivals, these gaudy occasions proliferate and always incorporate music. Predominately summertime occasions, some, like Reading and Donnington, have been going for years and provide an excellent means for seeing some of your favourite bands. Many take place in the open air, some are spectacular affairs including fireworks and light shows, featuring top opera stars. While street festivals are locality based, others are themed or culture based like **Africa Oyé**. Many are combined efforts. Liverpool's **Summer Pops** runs for two weeks, and the gamut, from children's choice to the choral experience.

Joining music societies

Football teams have their supporters' clubs and many divisions of the arts now rely on a little help from their friends. The benefits of joining a music society, especially for a reviewer, include:

- special discounts
- inclusion on the mailing list and regular newsletters
- free passes to open rehearsals
- opportunities to join an orchestra on foreign tours
- day trips to concerts and musical events.

ATTENDING A PRESS LAUNCH

With classical music, the hospitality is often the finest you will be fortunate

ROYAL LIVERPOOL PHILHARMONIC SOCIETY

Invites you to a launch of the

1996 SUMMER POPS

**at 12.00 noon in the Rodewald Suite
in the Peter Moores Wing
of the Philharmonic Hall**

on MONDAY 25 MARCH 1996

RSVP

Fig. 16. An invitation to a press call.

MONDAY

7–10am   It's Keith and Brian's Biggest Breakfast BONANZA!

10–12pm Time to talk with guest celebrity Elvira Henderson.

12–2pm   Loadsa fun at lunchtime with DJ Dave. Plus a look at what's happening this week entertainment wise.

2–6pm   Afternoon! It's The Auntie Jen Show with lots of fun chat and record requests. Plus the ten best selling records locally.

6–10pm   Jim's Night-time Nostalgia. Including: Art forum – or against 'em? Ring in and have your say! John Q. Smith will be here to answer your questions.

10–2am   Sit down and shut up! It's time for our stand-up comedy extravaganza. Send in your tape now! Plus cool sounds from your mate and ours, DJ Dave.

2–7am   Music all the way.

Fig. 17. A schedule for one day's radio programme.

enough to encounter. The press packs are lavish with detail but if you feel the accompanying photographs aren't suitable, alternative choices will be arranged. There is usually a display showing a mixture of past glories and future delights.

Serenaded by a string quartet, until the short speech of welcome describing forthcoming events, you are then regaled with a choice of first class red or white wine or orange juice, and invited to partake of a positively cornucopian spread. Even the coffee tastes every bit as delicious as it smells. In return, all you do is write a few kind words. Figure 16 is an example of an invitation.

WRITING THE REVIEW

Reviews of classical concerts follow the same lines as art. As does popular music; both reviews of CDs and gigs are usually considered fair game for comment ranging from gossip to insult. Unless written by fans, in which case the writing will assume a tone of the deepest reverence.

REVIEWING FOR LOCAL RADIO

Since no other medium makes as much use of music as the radio, this looks like the right place to discuss reviewing on the airways. It is nowhere near as easy as sitting down and writing reviews, and some people will find it nerve-wracking. But, like most things, you may like it once you've tried it. It's all experience.

Community radio is becoming so popular that as soon as the 28 day licence expires for one station, another one goes on the air. Usually a showcase, it offers opportunities for as many people as possible. Some of them will welcome the chance to put into practice all they have learned on training courses about production, working as a sound engineer and so on. Given the choice, most people fancy having a go at presenting – though there is rather more work involved in this than is often appreciated, especially as a successful presenter makes things sound too easy for words.

Radio makes a lot of use of listings and welcomes reviewers, since they can give the listener a good idea of what's worth going along to. A review section will usually be slotted in with another show and might last about half an hour, interspersed with records. Or it may be done as a forum, with everyone sitting round a table, offering different views. This is an easier set-up for your first time – if you don't feel like opening your mouth, nobody is going to notice. Figure 17 shows a schedule for one day's radio programme.

Solving possible problems

If you're not sure about reviewing on the air, have a think about your telephone manner. Providing you have no qualms about ringing anybody up and can chat away happily, then really, it's no different in a radio studio. You forget about the unlimited number of people tuning in and concentrate on talking to just one person, as if having a conversation with a friend.

The other main worry is going totally blank when you should be holding forth on the best gig in town or the most enjoyable concert. It is possible to prepare the review and simply read it aloud but it won't sound right. It's simpler to pick out keywords and use them as an *aide-memoire,* to jog your memory. Other than that, all you need do is keep a close eye on the presenter and be guided by her cues: when to start speaking, when to pause, when to sign off.

CASE STUDIES

Dexter finds he can't call the tune

Dexter approaches a top music magazine to ask if he could review classical CDs. They want to see the latest copy of the magazine but it doesn't give by-lines, there's just a list of contributors. However, the name of each sub-editor is in italic, as Katrina suggested, to make it easier for readers to find out who to approach if they want to write for the magazine. Otherwise, there is no proof of authorship: 'We're all in this together' beams the editor. Dexter can't even ask him to send a fax because he's meant to be too busy to write for other magazines.

Brent hits the high spot

Brent is asked to do a phone interview with the lead singer of a new band which is heavily tipped for the top. The record company have rung up at a ridiculously late hour and nobody else in the office can do it. At least Brent knows about the band, they've been plastered all over the papers lately, much to his annoyance; they are nowhere near as good as his lot, '*Qute*'. To his surprise, he and the singer end up getting on very well, though they spend more time discussing horror movies and UFOs than music. As the singer rings off, he tells Brent to send a demo down to the recording company.

Katrina is doomed to discord

Katrina is in Brent's good books at the moment so she takes the opportunity to ask him to let her do an interview with a band she really likes so that she can get into the gig for free. However, although she thought to ask for directions to get to the venue, she can't find the way in when she arrives nor anyone around to ask. Once inside, the band has to be interviewed in the gents, the only place which is quiet enough. And after the interview, the bouncer won't let her into the gig because her name is not on the guest list.

DISCUSSION POINTS

1. Are there many opportunities locally for reviewing music?

2. How would you find out about doing reviews on radio or television?

3. Do you feel qualified to do reviews in this area? If not, where do you learn more about it?

ASSIGNMENT

Pick one kind of music you really cannot abide and write a short review which would appeal to an avid fan.

7
Getting into Performance

This chapter discusses modern day theatre:

- how to learn more about all aspects of the performing arts
- involving yourself locally
- attending press calls
- writing the review.

DISCUSSING WHAT PERFORMANCE MEANS TODAY

Performance now includes all kinds of things besides plays:

- dance
- mime
- circus skills and physical theatre
- cabaret
- comedy
- musicals.

In London, as Jane Morris of the Society of London Theatre points out: 'Audiences during the week visit the theatre like they would the cinema. At the weekend, more people come into the city, making an occasion of it.'

Theatre Magazine recently confirmed in its readership survey that 81.8 per cent go to West End theatres, as well as those in their own and neighbouring regions. 86.9 per cent visit the theatre at least once a month; 71.4 per cent are over 35; 55.6 per cent over 55. Although for young people, constraints are often financial, it does argue the case for more new productions. Even with ballet, 'they tend to turn out for the old war-horses', rather than a new creation like David Bintley's *Far From the Madding Crowd.*

Public opinion counts

Musicals might not be to everybody's taste (never mind the quality, just listen to this tune) but they come top, attracting 83.8 per cent; classic drama (including 'A' level texts, presumably): 79.5 per cent; modern plays: 78.8 per cent; modern comedy: 65.6 per cent. So whatever anyone's idea of a good night out, they are quite evenly divided.

Venues are no longer confined to the traditional theatre, especially for amateur productions:

- town halls and community halls, even foyers
- colleges and schools
- museums and galleries
- café bars, pubs and clubs
- car parks and swimming pools
- city centres and parks.

Drama sometimes has a role to play in other settings, such as the business world, for psychological/therapeutic purposes or training sessions (customer services).

GETTING TO KNOW LOCAL VENUES

The average town or city will have at least one major venue, with maybe a couple of smaller theatres and one place designated as 'fringe', technically a studio, which holds audiences of less than 100. Each theatre will be known for a particular programme, the major venue playing host to the most spectacular productions:

- Andrew Lloyd Webber musicals which bring in the charabancs
- opera
- ballet
- musicals
- regional tours of West End hits
- regional premières.

Regional theatre is traditionally used for the debut of productions which then transfer to the West End – or not, as the case may be. Sometimes there are long-running productions, sometimes one-nighters. The programme may provide a wide variety of events besides plays: comedy evenings, musicals, concerts, or local drama and community groups. The aim is always to try and please most of the people most of the time.

Studios and fringe theatre are where you are more likely to come across experimental drama, by 'exciting new writers', making the most of their 'outstanding new talent' (and who have talked a friend into writing their press releases). Nevertheless, short of starring yourself in a major success story, the next best thing for any reviewer is to uncover genius.

FINDING OUT MORE

The idea of acting or playwriting may be anathema to you but you can still love drama. Neither is an encyclopaedic knowledge of every great drama required – wouldn't it be wonderful to attend a performance of *Hamlet* knowing nothing at all about it? It says something for the power of Shakespeare that nearly the whole world has heard of the Prince of Denmark. And what if all you know is from the two of his plays you did at 'A' Level? You are very unlikely ever again to study anything in as much depth; even a degree course is not as intensive because it covers so much more.

The simplest way to learn is by going to watch – this is why people write plays. Drama fascinates because each production can be interpreted differently.

Reading all about it

There are no courses specifically on reviewing but if some appear interesting, you can start educating yourself while waiting to apply. There are plenty of guides covering the major plays, full of information and useful notes (see the Further Reading section).

Admittedly, you don't often settle down with a good play and unless thoroughly curious, you could spend all your time writing theatre reviews without reading a single one. An easy way to start learning is:

- Sit at home and watch the delights television has in store.

- Check the listings and see what productions are on.

As some of these may be adapted from novels, the way it is done will clarify the potential of theatre. Likewise, with the book of the film, some people will argue that you should look at the book first, others, the film.

Consulting the experts

You can learn a lot from some reviewers: *eg* Jack Tinker in *The Mail*, and Michael Billington and Robin Thornber in *The Guardian*. There aren't very many female critics, as is the case with film.

Perusing reviews becomes even more interesting once you have your own published and can compare notes. Very interesting, if you happen to totally disagree. There are also magazines devoted to the stage, in particular, *Theatre Record*. This contains reviews from the national newspapers covering a large number of plays (mostly in London, but some regional). It provides an excellent opportunity to make comparisons – what the different critics have to say about a production, and *how* they say it. See the Further Reading section for other books and magazines.

Going on courses

This need not be very expensive, even if you are unwaged; sometimes courses are well under £2 a session, for example: The Workers Educational Association's (WEA) course on enjoying literature. Well, while you're at it, you may as well brush up on the novel and poetry, since it only covers a couple of plays. The further education programme includes classes which are more drama orientated and you may be eligible for accreditation:

- political theatre in Britain 1900–1995
- Irish literature today
- theatre playwright's workshop.

There are courses in modern classics, plus a number of day schools which deal with Shakespeare 'A' level texts. Theatres themselves often offer an education programme and occasional residencies, guided tours or open days, giving you the chance to have a look round and talk to the staff.

The education programme serves various purposes:

- community linked *ie* youth theatre, dance companies, reminiscence groups
- in association with schools and colleges for 'A' level students
- workshops with touring companies.

Workshops cover everything to do with theatre:

- directing and rehearsing
- production and design
- music and the theatre
- power status and control (physical exercises and improvisation)
- taking the text to the stage.

They might be run by the directors, or involve rehearsed readings, performance poetry, after show discussion, seminars, debates, physical theatre or script writing, sometimes culminating in a showcase. Many of these are aimed at children and young people, who are regarded as the audience and performers of the future. There are also workshops for teachers of English, drama and theatre studies, and programmes may include multi-skilled events, exploring techniques of drama, dance, mime and music. An example of a theatre education programme can be seen in Figure 18.

5-9 Hope Street, Liverpool L1 9BH
Telephone: 0151 708 0338
Facsimile: 0151 709 0398
Box Office: 0151 709 4776

EVERYMAN THEATRE EDUCATION DEPARTMENT
LISTINGS
SPRING 1996

Method & Madness

30 January After-show Talk
Mike Alfreds, Artistic Director of Method & Madness, talks about the company's methods and inspirations.
31 January 10 - 12 am Workshop for Teachers
Mike Alfreds leads a workshop for teachers of English, Drama and Theatre Studies on the company's techniques, focusing on the influence of Stanislavski on their work. This workshop is free for teachers and will take place in the auditorium.

Frankie & Tommy

14 & 28 February 4.30 - 6.30 pm Workshop
A workshop for GCSE and Alevel pupils led by Peter Rowe, Artistic Director of the Everyman Theatre and Director of 'Frankie & Tommy', exploring the production from the perspective of the director with a participatory workshop featuring Ben Fox ('Frankie') - bestknown to us all as Wishee-Washee from this year's sell-out 'wok 'n' roll' Everyman panto, 'Aladdin'.
15 & 29 February 5.30 - 6.30 pm Workshop
An introduction to production and design with the crew of the Everyman production of 'Frankie & Tommy'. This behind-the-scenes look at the inner workings of the theatre is designed for GCSE and Alevel Drama and Theatre Studies pupils.
16 February After-show Talk
Garry Lyons, acclaimed writer of 'Frankie & Tommy', and the son of Frankie Lyons, Tommy Cooper's long-lost double act partner, will be coming up to Liverpool to see the production and talk to audiences about his relationship with his father and his reasons for writing the play.
21 February 4.30 - 6.30 pm Workshop
As 14 February, for students and other adults.
22 February 5.30 - 6.30 pm Workshop
As 15 February, for students and other adults.

Artistic Director Peter Rowe
Administrative Director Kevin Fearon
Chair of the Board Jane Winter
Honorary Director Terry Hands

New Everyman Limited
Registered in England and Wales No 2883510
Registered Office 5-9 Hope Street L1 9BH
Registered Charity 1040257 VAT No 618 7839 94

Fig. 18. Everyman Theatre education programme.

Kaboodle

5 March After-show Talk
Lee Beagley, Artistic Director of the Liverpool-based company, Kaboodle productions talks about the company and their production of Euripides' classic Greek tragedy, 'The Bacchae'.
7 March 2.00 - 4.00 pm Workshop
A workshop for music students, led by award-winning actor-director, Lee Beagley, along with composer-performers, George Ricci and Andy Frizzell.
8 March 2.00 - 4.00 pm Workshop
Theatre Styles: essential insight for students of Theatre Studies and Drama, this participatory workshop will explore the development of theatre from its beginnings in Greek Theatre.

Scottish Dance Theatre

11 March After-show Talk
Neville Campbell, ex-director of the critically acclaimed Phoenix Dance Company and now Artistic Director of Scottish Dance Theatre talks about the company's new production of 'Human Tales'.

Levi Tafari & Adrian Henri

19 & 20 March 9.30 - 1.00 and 2.00 - 4.00 pm Workshops and performances
Two of Liverpool's most highly-acclaimed and best loved poetic voices, Adrian Henri and Levi Tafari are offering exclusive workshops and performances for children aged 10-13 for 2 days only at the Everyman Theatre. Morning sessions will take the form of participatory workshops where children have the opportunity to learn about and try their hand at two very different styles of poetry. During the afternoons, Levi and Adrian will be performing an exclusive double-act of poetry.

Barrie Rutter & Blake Morrison

21 March 6.00 pm Reading
The two staunch Yorkshire men present another coup for the Everyman Theatre - a reading from Blake Morrison's 'When Did You Last See Your Father?' and 'The Ballad of the Yorkshire Ripper'.

Death & the Maiden

10 April 4.30 - 6.30 pm Workshop
A study of power, status and control relationships in the play by means of participatory physical improvisations and exercises, for students and other adults.
11 April 5.30 - 6.30 pm Workshop
A tour-demonstration focusing on the technical aspects of the production, including lighting, design and sound.
16 & 17 April 4.30 - 6.30 pm Workshop
As 10 April, for GCSE and Alevel students.
18 & 19 April 5.30 - 6.30 pm Workshop
As 11 April, for GCSE and Alevel students.

Tours of the theatre are also available for groups on request.

FOR MORE INFORMATION ABOUT TIMES AND AVAILABILITY, CONTACT CATHERINE WILLIAMS, EDUCATION OFFICER OR BRIAN PARKES, PRESS & MARKETING OFFICER AT THE EVERYMAN THEATRE ON 0151 708 0338.

Fig. 18. Continued.

BECOMING INVOLVED

If you decide to concentrate on theatre reviews, it can be immensely valuable to understand more about what goes on behind the scenes, by:

- helping out in local theatres
- joining a drama group
- performing yourself.

Most theatres are so hard up they welcome volunteers; the jobs which should prove to be most helpful for a reviewer are research to help compile the programme and marketing.

The regional arts board newsletter is full of information – investigating sponsorship might be useful, or attending conferences. Awards are always available, often offering substantial amounts of money; many people are not even aware of this, meaning you are up against less competition.

Building up your confidence

As far as a spot of DIY goes, by now you should be acquainted with some of the local groups; they, too, are always grateful for extra (unpaid) help. From taking over the prompter's job to helping out by trying to beg, steal or borrow props, it may not be such a gigantic leap to making your debut in the spotlight. If you prefer to build up your confidence first, and you're fed up peering at yourself in the mirror, there are always courses and workshops:

- finding your voice
- actors' workshop
- practical drama from page to stage.

Drama does wonders for your self-confidence, something a freelance needs absolutely oodles of, for making new contacts and making the most of opportunities – and for dealing with rejection. If this is something which has you crying yourself to sleep at night – have you considered that freelancing may not be for you? And as far as dramatic irony is concerned, if you are somewhat venomous when reviewing – the words 'glass houses' and 'stones' come to mind.

If freelancing keeps you busy and successful, before long you'll see it's a waste of time worrying about being rejected. Not that you shouldn't do your best to learn from your mistakes, but there's no need to brood over them.

ATTENDING PRESS CALLS

Not all theatres go in for **press calls**; when they do, it can be for a variety of reasons:

● To promote their latest production.

● To announce the new season's programme.

● To gain maximum publicity for future plans, particularly if this involves funding (to prevent the theatre closing or making a lottery application).

It may also be to help guarantee advance bookings. When Tommy Steele toured with *What a Show!*, invitations went to every organisation who might be interested. Making himself approachable meant interviews throughout the media 'publicising the production' plus a whole new lot of fans.

Even if you are concentrating on reviews, take advantage of these invitations when possible since background information gives you greater insight into the play itself.

Press packs can range quite widely, from a single sheet of A4 containing the CV of the leading performer plus a photograph, to what appear to be the lavishly illustrated proofs of their latest autobiography.

Press calls are sometimes on a rota basis, where everyone gets their ten minutes of coming close to fame, chatting with a megastar. More often though, they take the form of a general question and answer session. Here, the novice can just sit and concentrate on what everyone else is saying.

WRITING THE REVIEW

Basically your review should consist of: a description of the set; what the play is about; the various performances. And even if you do have a wide frame of reference ('of course, the absolutely definitive *Hamlet* just had to be Larry – seminal performance, seminal . . . '), odds are space won't permit you to display your erudition, *ie* show off.

Agents provide photos of the performers while shots of them in action are sometimes available from the theatre.

Monthly magazines don't often use theatre reviews, apart from long-running performances like pantomimes, which are invariably put on for at least a month at Christmas (oh yes they are! Sorry, couldn't resist it). They even put in an appearance during school holidays. Summer shows, aimed at attracting tourists, are often staged for about six weeks, although many theatres close during August.

However, a review can be rewritten to preview something which has been on before, and there is an argument for including touring productions – *The Rocky Horror Show* has been wandering around the country now for over 21 years.

CASE STUDIES

Dexter thinks life is a drag

Dexter has to do a last minute interview with top comedy drag artiste, Dolly Daydream, but can't get hold of him. He decides to make it up, turning the facts from the press pack into conversation. Next afternoon, the phone rings. Lucky for Dexter, Dolly has a sense of humour; unluckily, he is asked to read the 'interview' out but Dolly is very impressed. Then they discover they're from the same town. Eventually, Dexter tries out a few of his jokes. They're not that funny (it's the way he tells them) but Dolly asks him to drop him a line because he uses up loads of material.

Brent's very own melodrama

Brent swaps with Katrina so he can see a production that one of this mates in starring in. It's so badly organised there isn't even a spare programme, but they can provide him with a cast list for the review. The play is really awful; he starts writing notes in the interval and says afterwards not to worry about the cast list: 'To protect the innocent – I won't reveal the names'. He is overheard by the publicist, who at first seems to appreciate Brent's kindly offer of feedback, but then objects to this attitude. They end up fighting, and are barred from the theatre.

Katrina discovers the meaning of dramatic irony

Katrina keeps receiving press releases from a local theatre group. They're well written and eye-catching; curious, she goes to watch them in rehearsal and ends up doing an interview about their next production. This is on for just one night because that's all they can afford, even in the smallest theatre. Their future plans are well thought out and she is sure they will be a success; she tells them a piece will go in to publicise the play. But there's no space – the editor decides to have a double-page spread on the 60s popstar making his seventeenth come-back.

DISCUSSION POINTS

1. What type of performance appeals to you most? Is it worth specialising in this area?

2. How far are you prepared to become involved with theatre? What kind of obstacles are you likely to meet up with?

3. Do you think it may open up other possibilities?

ASSIGNMENT

Pick an area you know well and write a 200 word review criticising it. Compare with a favourable review of the same length on something you are new to.

8
Looking at Film and Video

This chapter discusses how to review films and videos, looking at:

- the role of videos and films as an art form
- learning more
- making contacts
- working for local media
- writing the review.

MAKING MOVIES

Cinema, even though celebrating its centenary this year, is the baby of the arts. A child of the technological age, it also differs in other ways from the rest of the arts and is perhaps the most glamorous. The heartfelt cry of the ambitious (if not necessarily the gifted) is: 'I want to be a star!' *ie* film star. The expression **superstar** was probably first associated with the stage production *Jesus Christ Superstar,* then swiftly applied to people like Barbra Streisand, followed by the likes of Elton John and stand-up comedians. Now, anyone who is quite good at anything is termed a superstar.

Cinema has always been the most accessible art form – anyone can go to the pictures. In the early days, cinema goers found themselves in the sumptuous surroundings of fabulous Art Deco picture palaces, so different to their home environment.

Theatre, classical music and art are often regarded as pursuits for the middle and upper classes, as literature once was; the working class could rarely afford books and were frequently unable to read them. Yet video was included as one of life's little necessities in a recent report on poverty. Sitting in your own home watching your favourite film, whether hired or taped, is no longer seen as a luxury. As for television, it solves the argument about theatre versus cinema by bridging the gap, bringing them together via the same medium.

The role of video and film

Videos give you the option of choosing exactly what you want to see. They are cheap and convenient . . . but it's not quite the same as going out to the pictures. American writer, Susan Sontag, in her essay in *The Guardian* on the centenary of cinema, says that the audience 'wanted to be kidnapped by the movie', a somewhat menacing metaphor, though 'transported' isn't much of substitute.

She also says: 'Cinema, once heralded as *the* art of the 20th century, seems now . . . to be a decadent art.' Cinema undoubtedly has a profound effect on its audience. It is frequently criticised for encouraging sex and violence, as well as exploitation (not to mention spin-off merchandise). However, cinema is still the greatest means of escapism, like travel. With film and video, we can believe that all things are possible and maybe this is what accounts for their continuing popularity with all classes and all ages.

READING UP AND LEARNING MORE

The library will have a copy of *Screen International Euroguide 95: Guide to Film, TV and Video in Europe* – all the information about studios, distributors, publications and so on. There is also the classic *Halliwell's Film Guide*, as well as news stand magazines. *Flicks* is free of charge in the cinema but appears to be made up of press releases. Some literary magazines contain a section on film – the final seal of respectability as a genuine art form.

What courses are available?

Once again, there is not a wide choice of courses, despite the number of people who want to learn what goes on behind a camera, never mind assessing the finished result on the screen. It's invariably tied up with other things under the multimedia umbrella (presumably by virtue of its modernity), and not regarded in the same light as the traditional arts. Even LIPA does not seem to run a specific course; acting is under theatre studies. Other courses are fairly esoteric: Women in Film and Television, or ambiguous: Visual Production.

Film and video also appear under creative writing:

- an introduction to videography
- an introduction to film theory
- video workshop.

The Savage Club has recently been set up to showcase regional, national and international artists working in performance art, live art and film and video.

Film societies and festivals

There are film societies to be found in most towns and usually an independent cinema which shows classics of the genre rather than the latest release; the local concert hall may include films in its programme.

Other festivals which included film events are held in Brighton, Bury St Edmunds and Canterbury; one venue definitely worth a visit is the Museum of Photography, Film and Television in Bradford.

MAKING CONTACTS

Films, of course, appear nationwide. So, unlike theatre, you are not restricted to the local press. Yet, being very popular, especially amongst student writers, reviewing films and videos can be difficult to get into. Attending press shows, you soon realise what an enormous pool of critics each university must possess.

Solving possible problems

It can be difficult to make contacts as an independent reviewer since you are assumed to be reviewing on behalf of a specific publication. Where videos are concerned, because there is a huge turnover, you are unlikely to be able to get hold of anything other than current releases, even if you have convinced your editor that 'cult corner' is the readers' choice.

Like art, the film industry is big business and frequently something of a closed shop. In this country, even the greatest of superstars is usually available for interview when their latest film is due out – no publicity is a frightening thing. However, American stars are a different kettle of fish altogether. They may visit this country for promotional purposes, but this entails sharing a sofa with 'Richard n' Judy' or other top name interviewers, not sparing five minutes to chat to some eager beaver teenager over the phone. By and large, they are inaccessible to any Tom, Dick or Harry – unless T., D. or H. happen to be famous reviewers.

Dealing with the distributors

All the main distributors are based in London, which seems to keep them out of touch with the rest of the world. They will insist on seeing a copy of the magazine, plus a fax (or a letter, if you *must* depend on such a primitive form of communication) from the editor containing your details for their mailing list. Yet not all of them insist on having a look at your published work.

Although that initial video might prove hard to prise out of them, generally speaking, they will then readily agree to provide tickets, promotional material and videos as readers' offers and competition prizes. See Figure 19 which is an example of a video competition.

It can be a very long-winded process, but it's the only way to do it – other than reworking your film reviews. With films, whilst awaiting the

COMPETITION TIME

We have copies of EVERY video featued on this page to give away as prizes. Just take a look at the questions below and send in the answers for the tapes you would like to win. There will be a separate draw for each title.

To win a copy of:

Interview With The Vampire - Name the author of Dracula

The Specialist - Name <u>two</u> Sharon Stone films.

Circle Of Friends - Which character did Chris O'Donnell play in Batman Forever?

Clockwork Mice - Land and Freedom is about which war?

Maverick - Name one other James Garner film.

Death Warrant - Which country is Van Damme from?

Hard To Kill - Name Segal's character in Under Siege.

Due South - What is the name of Fraser's dog?

World's Funniest Commercials - Who fronts the John Smith ad campaign?

Mark Little Sucks Live! - Name Joe Mangel's dog from Neighbours.

Potty Time - Name any of Bentine's fellow Goons.

The First American Teenager - "What make of car was Dean driving when he died?."

Craig Charles Live on Earth - Tell us the name of Charles' character in Red Dwarf.

All answers should be sent on a postcard, to Bumper Video Giveaway, The Guide, 260 Picton Road, Wavertree, L15 4LP. Please specify which video(s) you are attempting to win.

Fig. 19. Video competition in *The Guide*.

official seal of approval, you can start by contacting your local cinema to find out about press shows. They will usually agree to let you attend because, as a reviewer, you will already know at least some of the small, select band of regulars and that should be sufficient to provide your *bona fides*.

WORKING FOR LOCAL MEDIA

Here, your kind offer to provide reviews may be accepted because there are so many films and not usually enough staff to cover even the most popular releases. Unfortunately, they are more likely to decline through lack of space. Even if they do include reviews, careful study often makes it clear that the writer hasn't been within a million miles of the cinema, but simply obtained the details from the press release. This can be very entertaining when it's the one and only review praising a film universally acknowledged as a complete waste of celluloid.

A safer bet is local radio, particularly community radio, always keen to encourage people to participate and to keep their listeners informed about what's going on locally. With listings magazines, one film editor reckons to include approximately 20 films each month, which gives some indication of the demand.

It is also worth looking at small/independent press magazines, some of which occasionally have a film section. If not, there's no harm in your suggesting it, especially if it's a publication for whom you are already working.

ATTENDING A PRESS SHOW

Film reviews, like theatre, have two purposes: to encourage the reader to visit a particular cinema or to see a particular film. Having your reviews appear in the local press is the best way to keep the cinema manager happy, but if this is not possible, you need to look further afield.

Another consideration is the frequency of publication. The daily paper may include several film reviews each week while local radio provides even more coverage, with an entertainment roundup several times each day. Magazines also appear fortnightly, monthly, bi-monthly and quarterly. But for everybody who has to be the first in the queue, there are always plenty who take time to make their mind up and miss out on this honeymoon period; it could be your review which persuades them in the end.

Fortunately, with multi-screen cinemas, a wide range of films are on offer at one time, the most popular for up to six months. Yet the press show is often just before the film is released, maybe a week in advance, which gives you hardly any leeway. Worse still, they can be transferred to another cinema at the last minute, or even cancelled.

'Quite unbelievable': *Daily Splurge*

'Has to be seen to be believed': *Vivandi*

'Wouldn't go that far.': *Go for it!*

DEVILLE PRODUCTIONS
presents

A John Q. Smith Production

Blue Swayed
Starring Elvira Henderson

Co-starring Jez Carradine, as her manager

Guest appearance: Lynette Henderson, as Elvira's mother
Special guest appearance: Elouise Henderson,
as her long lost sister
Very special guest appearance:
Jez Henderson, as Elouise's missing baby son

With 37 new songs.

Fig. 20. Cover of a film press pack.

Who's who of reviewers

Typical reviewers are from the local papers, local radio (some representing popular taste, others, your actual film buff), listings magazines and student magazines: perhaps as many as a dozen people, sometimes as few as two. Occasionally, people with less obvious connections will turn up: independent cinema managers, magazine editors who are fans of particular movie stars, or people researching books.

Since the film critics are the experts, the post-cinematic gathering in the bar is often as useful as watching the film itself, let alone reading the press pack – if it turns up on time (and whatever you've just seen, it is always the best film ever made).

Press packs come in all shapes and sizes, from a set of faintly photocopied A4 sheets stapled together to a hefty booklet, even what appears to be one of those very expensive pop-up birthday cards. Sometimes they dwell on the story behind the film sometimes how the film was made, and there are always huge biographies of the stars. Figure 20 is an example of a press pack cover.

One word of warning – film reviewers tend to be male and with all that sex and violence and propensity for exploitation of the fair sex, ardent feminists may prefer to give this area a miss. Unless, of course, they are possessed of a heartfelt crusading spirit. Just to balance the books, it is worth noting that literature often bows down to the demands of the politically correct, as does theatre.

WRITING THE REVIEW

Film reviews differ from theatre mainly because they invariably tell the story, if only as a brief résumé; with drama, the reader is generally assumed to have some idea about the production, unless it is a brand new play. Film reviewers may have a day job as actor, director, producer or student, but again, this can often be a fruitful area for the amateur. However, as usual, no going into detail and ruining the effects of the special effects.

The review will also remark on the leading roles and how well or otherwise they were portrayed, but restrict comment on the rest of the cast to up and coming talent. There's usually the proverbial cast of thousands whereas most plays are limited to a maximum of eight players, giving you space for at least one adjective per person. Directors are becoming more renowned: Ridley Scott and Renny Harlin, for example, and their technique may also be mentioned, as will the settings and structure. Stills (photos of the stars) and action shots from the film are readily available. See Figure 21 for an example of two film reviews.

Where videos are concerned, reviews are pared down to a minimal description, topped off with some pithy summing up.

Film: Toy Story; *RATING ?* NB CHECK RELEASE DATES + SPELLING !

We have the technology! Er, now what do we do with it? Well, it's worth the wait because this is the happiest of marriages between the latest and the old-fashioned. It's odd, however, the way 'real people' end up as cardboard characters, especially where Mom and kids get on just great and Sid, the child who creates hell, can leap out of bed at 8.00am. There are sly digs at PC, some wonderful in-jokes, but - no Dads? And how come the average American family always lives in a huge house? *MENTION VOICE-OVERS - TOM HANKS AS WOODY, ETC*

Never mind. Every child has toys with lives of their own - a dinosaur who is a nervous wreck (never mind Bo Peep)? But this is dream come true plus some quite nightmarish sequences. And although the various morals are didactic, again as is usual with US productions, it still understands that all children own T Shirts proclaiming 'It's not fair' on the front and 'it's not my fault' on the back and deftly handles their worst fears of being rejected and/or bullied. This is really too good for kids. You'll come out wishing you knew all the words to the James Brown hit, but the title will do: ' I feel GOOD!'.

Film: *Cut-Throat Island -* *COLD RATING ?*

Well, this certainly is an incredible film, a case not so much of suspending disbelief as let it go hang altogether. It'd have Errol Flynn leaping out of his grave with one bound. Scuttled together from every pirate film ever made: map of missing treasure, treachery (there's at least half a dozen villains, though Frank Langella does manage to outshine them all). Geena Davis as Pirate Princess Feisty aka Morgan is all bosom and balls - poor old Mathew Modine is just no match for all his charm and wit.

Action-packed full to bursting, blood and guts in all directions, chockfull of every cliche in the book. Yes, of all these things but the trouble is, it destroys the tension because you know they'll get out of every scrape. Okay, it's quite stunning to look at, what with all the special effects and all (everything gets blown up - out of proportion), but whenever anyone opens their mouth - DIRElogue. Oh dear me. Nice picture, shame about the movie.

3

PHOTOS - HAS EDITOR ARRANGED THIS ?

IF NOT, PHONE DISTRIBUTER (NO IN PRESS PACK OR RING CINEMA)

Fig. 21. An example of a draft for two film reviews.

CASE STUDIES

Dexter could use some special effects

Dexter makes his first trip to the cinema, and has planned to meet the film editor outside – but there's no sign of him. In fact, there's no sign of life in the cinema. Well, he is a bit early (20 minutes early in fact). Eventually, a smartly suited man arrives, and presses the door bell to the side of the entrance. Dexter tries to explain who he is but clearly, he is not believed; besides, there is no press show scheduled. Later that same day, back in the office, the exasperated film editor wants to know where Dexter got to – he'd been in the other cinema, the one round the corner.

Brent . . . testing, testing, one, two, three

Brent shares the editor's vision of the possibilities of Cable TV; the magazine has been loaned some very expensive equipment from a local recording studio, in return for setting up training courses to encourage students to script programmes for community radio. So Brent sort of borrows it one evening to do a promo of *Qute* in action. But none of the band have a clue how it works (and can't really ask anyone's advice) so the session takes three times as long to record as expected. Nobody thinks to check the sound levels – nice picture, shame you can't actually hear them.

Katrina reviews films for the radio

Katrina is talked into doing some film reviews for the local radio station as Brent has made himself scarce. Besides, he prefers TV; nobody can see you on the radio. Katrina doesn't mind, she loves the cinema but never seems to get the opportunity to go. But it turns out to be very time consuming: watching the films, writing about them, going up to the studio at the other end of town. She has attended all the planning meetings but practice obliterates theory; it mostly goes haywire and Katrina finds herself hanging around for hours waiting to go on and do her bit.

DISCUSSION POINTS

1. If your most secret ambition is to be a filmstar, will reviewing come in useful?

2. Do you enjoy going to the cinema so much you find you have a very low critical threshold?

3. What about working on the radio? Or even in television?

ASSIGNMENT

Pick a recent review you violently disagree with and give your reasons for refuting it – on a purely critical basis *ie* without casting aspersions.

9
Making the Most of Leisure

Leisure includes tourist attractions, restaurants, events and festivals and travel. Travel writing incorporates much of what is required when describing leisure activities. Written as a review, it is usually regarded as an article or a feature, due to the length, and is one of the most popular topics. Clearly, for many freelances, there's just something *so* romantic about travel writing, and this chapter starts by taking a close look at it:

● Is travel writing for you?

● How to work out what editors require.

Then we look at writing restaurant reviews:

● making the arrangements
● and writing up the review.

STUDYING TRAVEL WRITING

Reviewing tourist attractions is an excellent start. However, watch out for any adverts which assure you there is 'A secret way to pay for all your travel'. The travel industry is a tightly knit network and anyone working a scam *ie* inventing assignments in order to get all expenses paid trips, especially abroad, will soon be found out. The only travelling they end up doing is right up the garden path.

Selling your work
There are various outlets for writing about different leisure activities:

● newspapers (local and national): columns or articles
● magazines: women's interest, lifestyle and travel
● speciality magazines: activity; sport; wildlife.

Books
- guidebooks
- coffee table collections: an artbook depicting creatures in the wild
- special interest: essential first aid for rock climbers.

Other possibilities
- brochures
- press releases
- advertorials: features accompanying advertisements – 'health farm of the month' (see Figure 22).

TRAVELLING HOPEFULLY

Fired by enthusiasm at tackling this genre, now is the time to ask yourself a few pertinent questions. They also apply to other leisure activities:

1. Is this sort of writing likely to be right up your street?

2. Would you prefer to go for the soft option, writing about less strenuous leisure activities?

3. Do you want to explore your spirit of adventure?

4. Do you really enjoy travelling? Are you enthusiastic, curious, patient, persistent?

5. Is your health good?

6. And your manners? Any behaving badly means no more invites, whereas a good reputation helps with networking.

7. Have you actually got time to travel? Part-time (the occasional trip, once a month or a week at a time?), full-time (several weeks away). It is *not* advisable to start off trying to do this full-time.

8. Do you possess other useful abilities *eg* motivation and organisation; research and marketing skills?

9. Do you have plenty of self-confidence? Travel writing can be difficult to get into and you have to be able to approach editors, hotel-owners and the like, plus dealing with rejections and being let down.

10. Other skills required: languages, geography, history and photography

Health & Fitness Special

life's a beach for ....Mr Motivator

CINDY CRAWFORD, eat your heart out! You may look sexier in lycra but, when it comes to making fitness videos that sell, Derrick Evans is in a league of his own

Derrick who?

Don't worry you do know him, or at least you know his screen persona, for Derrick is none other than GMTV's Mr Motivator!

As Mr M he has sold more fitness videos this decade than Britain has sold arms to Iraq. His last effort, the classily titled BLT (Bums, Legs and Tums) has been in the fitness and sports video chart for a staggering one hundred weeks and counting

He's certainly come a long way from his early days as Eammon Holmes and Lorraine Kelly's personal trainer. Today he lists Hollywood celebrities such as Danny Glover (Lethal Weapon) and Luther Vandross among his clients. Not bad for a Jamaican boy who didn't even come to England until he was 10 years old.

The 'Guide' decided to find out what Derrick's new video 'Mr Motivator's 10 Minute Workout' was all about, and Mr M was only too keen to explain 'The video is made up of six 10 minute workouts, there are three general sections and three specific workouts for the problem areas, the Bums, Legs and Tums, so you can do one or all of them, depending on how much time you have to spend'

The fact that Mr M went to St Lucia for filming certainly raised a few eyebrows Was this strictly necessary? 'You bet', comes the reply. 'the bare walls in a studio are not inspirational. Most exercise videos are boring, it's important to create the right environment, everyone wants to be in the sun and on the beach and you think to yourself yes I'd like to be there, it gives you something to aim for'

mr motivator's 10 MINUTE WORKOUTS

Apart from its exotic location what does Mr M think distinguishes his video from the millions of other releases cluttering the shelves at the moment? 'I could use the old cliché 'Forget the rest, buy the best ' he laughs 'but the most important thing with my videos is to have fun while you're exercising, you don't want to think 'Oh, still another two minutes to the end' It's important to create the right atmosphere, the music is important too, it needs to be something you'd tap your feet to' He went on, 'One of the most important things, I feel, is that the ladies used in the videos are a good representation of who would be working out with it, this isn't a video by a celebrity saying look this is how I got myself fit'

But how does he expect 10 minute workout to fare alongside BLT?

'The new one is 10 times better', he claims, 'there is no excuse with this one, you only need to find 10 minutes, this one will be in the charts for 200 weeks!'

What is Mr M looking forward to in 1996 then 'I'm pleased with the way my life's going at the moment so I'll hope for more of the same, and to remain healthy - I'm very rarely ill, long may this continue'

'Mr Motivator's 10 Minute Workouts', released by Polygram Video is available now, priced £10.99.

10 Things You Never Knew about Mr. Motivator

1 His real name is Derrick Evans
2 Mr M was born in Jamaica in the Caribbean and came to live in the UK when he was 10
3 He got the job at GMTV after being personal trainer to Lorraine Kelly and Eammon Holmes
4 Mr M is friends with singer Luther Vandross and has helped him achieve his new svelte look
5 He personally feels Fergie's new looks are purely down to diet and not exercise as she claims!
6 He used to personally train Gloria Hunniford and Paul Young
7 He once owned a Rottweiler, unfortunately it was stolen
8 He is currently learning to sing and play the piano
9 When he has any spare time, Mr Motivator likes to play squash and badminton
10 He has his head shaved once a week at his barber's in Willesden, London, where he has been going for over 22 years. The shop has seen him through his afro and curly perms to now.

Mr Motivator stocking up on his favourite videos!!

Fig. 22. An example of an advertorial.

in particular. Increasingly, editors are only interested in articles with photographs (and not just where travel writing is concerned). Promotional material is usually available.

11. Can you afford to invest in the right equipment: camera, laptop, tape recorder, notebook (with your name and local address on the cover) and pen.

Looking around your own backyard

'So how do I go about doing travel writing?' The answer is – right on the street where you live. Even if inhabiting a backwater, civilisation cannot be that far away. Admittedly, if your home town is known for its unspoilt loveliness, writing about it could put an end to that.

Where advertorials are concerned, if you come up with a good idea, a better one is to suggest it to a local publication since it means extra revenue for them through advertising sales. A picture may be worth a thousand words, an advertisement several more, but put them together with the feature you are writing about one particular company (or several) or event, and the resulting enquiries from the readership should keep everybody happy.

Remember not to let familiarity breed contempt since what is old hat to you can be new and exciting to everybody else.

Getting away from it all

There is a tremendous demand for articles on tourist activities because the world now is our oyster. As a writer, it's up to you to show off the pearls, mentally transporting the reader so they can appreciate all the delights. Bear in mind that while some will be content to visit in their imagination, others expect you to spell out any problems.

Many publications want an expert opinion to impress their readers; others prefer somebody's first hand experience so their readers decide, 'well, I bet we could do that too'. Overall, your writing should be entertaining and educational; you should be honest and objective, as well as lyrical in your descriptions, besides being practical in your advice.

Home from home

What is your area particularly known for? So many people are fascinated by local history, most libraries have 'snippets' box containing newspaper cuttings of interest to the community. Start keeping one of your own or arrange to have a look through theirs and photocopy the most interesting pieces. These should provide plenty of ideas and generate quite a few articles.

- famous landmarks
- anniversary celebrations

- local celebrities (people are fascinated by human interest stories)
- interesting developments
- award winning hotels, restaurants
- festivals, craft fairs, events.

Holidays and business trips

Another good start is to make the most of any suitable opportunity, especially if you're on a very small budget. If you've been writing for a magazine for some time and have a good relationship with the editor, they may let you loose in the area of travel writing. Sometimes there are monthly guidelines listing the areas to be covered, which gives you an idea of when best to try offering your services.

WRITING TO ORDER

Understanding what the editor is looking for

The most successful pieces are written from personal experience, are well researched and include all the necessary information. *Don't* include anything irrelevant *eg*, a feature about a deep sea fishing holiday needn't mention that paragliding used to be popular further up the coast.

Include local activities and amenities (hotels and restaurants), keeping in mind the appropriate price range of the readership, as well as their age group and interests. The style should be a combination of **informative** and **entertaining** but take it easy on the adjectives. The main text covers particular features and essential details:

- **What to expect**: good points (friendly service; scenery) plus problems like overcrowded beaches.

- **Eating out**: average cost of three course meal with wine; cost of beer/bottle of wine.

- **Late night venues**: likely cost; where to go; how to dress.

- **Shopping**: bargains and exclusive buys; markets and their specialities; souvenirs and cost.

- **Getting around**: taxi rates; local transport (buses, trains: how easy/efficient/regular; car rental.

- **Health**: temperatures and seasonal warnings; hospitals and doctors; any crime/security warnings.

Special requirements or priorities may include:

- families/singles/groups/disabled
- peace and quiet; activities; cultural visits; nightlife
- local customs and events
- tipping: how much and when.

Beginning at the beginning

Contact the appropriate tourist board for brochures; your local library will also have guidebooks, articles and encyclopaedias. Remember, research teaches you more, suggests ideas and shows you what stories have been done to death. Photocopy anything useful, like maps, and note handy addresses and contacts.

Who's writing the review?

All right, article then – the opening should catch the reader's attention and be balanced by an equally strong ending. Travel writing is often done in the first person, although there is an argument for using the third person to prevent writing from becoming ego-centric, causing a barrier. However, the third person can convey detachment and first person is preferred for a more friendly style, since it more easily recreates a situation. With practice, both styles can produce the required effect.

MAKING ARRANGEMENTS: RESTAURANT REVIEWS

You can usually follow this procedure whatever you're reviewing. Restaurant reviews can also be utilised as part of a series: speciality food, theme nights, family eating, special offers, even 'ladies who lunch'. But always allow plenty of time to organise it – don't be ringing up at 11.30am because you fancy something Mexican for lunch. And don't eat beforehand; with the demise of *nouvelle cuisine* (roughly translated as: where's my dinner got to?), portions nowadays tend to be bountiful. Figure 23 is an example of a restaurant review.

Having reservations?

A phone call or a visit should be sufficient to set it all up; there is a great deal of competition where eating out is concerned. The majority of managers will welcome the publicity and an interview, in return for a complimentary meal for two. If they demur, compromise by suggesting you 'do lunch' *ie* interview the manager during your complimentary meal.

Some restaurants have a policy which does not allow a free lunch – their success relies on word of mouth. This is the most effective means of promotion, possible because for many people, a meal out is for a special and

TAKE YOUR TIME AND PAMPER YOURSELF...

AT PASTIME RESTAURANT & BANQUETING SUITE
42 Hamilton Square, Birkenhead L41 5BP (647 8095)

Everybody's favourite - Pastime, which is hardly surprising, as it was established twenty years ago, and the food is fabulous. Absolutely!

While we perused the hefty menu, we were served with a dainty arrangement of canapes: cheese straws, vol-au-vents, and so on. But I'm afraid we both chickened out of sampling slices of Roast Ostrich, served with Pigeon (£12.50), though apparently it tastes like steak.

For the first course (£3.85), I went for that good old standby, Seafood Cocktail - not just prawns and sauce on a bed of lettuce and cucumber squeezed into an eye-glass, oh no, the plate was the size of a tray, lovingly decorated with lettuce curls and vegetable ornaments. My companion went for the Lambs Liver - NOT everybody's cup of tea...well, not anybody's, I suppose, since you can't drink it, but it was delicious, combined with chopped shallots, fresh herbs and marsala sauce.

After a small portion of delicious sorbet, on to the main course. Joy! My favourite, Steak Rossini (£12.95), which is wrapped in bacon, placed on a fried crouton, topped with pate, and coated with madeira sauce. My companion picked Venison Wellington (£11.75), served up in puff pastry with a chestnut stuffing and a poivrade sauce - a mouthful in every sense of the word. This was accompanied by potatoes (boiled, and sauteed with onions), and a technicolour vegetable platter.

On to dessert (£3.50): Chocolate Mushrooms for him, made out of white chocolate mousse topped with a chocolate meringue, and served with a chocolate anglaise. I had Deep Fried Ice Cream, coated in almond sponge and placed in a brandy snap basket, which for once really was melt-in-the-mouth, rather than risk-breaking-off-your-teeth. It usually comes with a walnut and raisin sauce, which I waived (much to my companion's annoyance; he'll eat anything); a note at the beginning of the menu assures you that food can be prepared to your liking.

Nearly three hours later, we withdrew to the Bar Lounge, to slump, sated, onto the sofa, after a meal which was THE most successful combination of presentation a la Nouvelle Cuisine AND portions to suit the heartiest appetite.

Must finish off with a thank you to the staff, some of whom were new, as they all did a really excellent job. So if you want a truly sumptuous evening, sampling scrumptious food, you know where to go to be sure of a really good time.

Carole Baldock

Fig. 23. An example of a restaurant review.

96

Fig. 24. A sample info panel.

hopefully, memorable occasion. Other restaurants can be awkward customers, insisting on a letter of confirmation from your editor or telling you
to contact their head office with a fax. It's up to you to decide whether this
is really worth pursuing.

Tucking in

Having arranged a convenient time for the meal, allow perhaps 20 minutes
beforehand to be shown round and to chat to the manager, having prepared
a few questions in advance.

If offered a courtesy drink, remember alcohol can impair your judge-
ment so don't plump for a triple brandy. Nor is this the time to decide to go
on that diet. Ask for a menu and any leaflets; the former will act as an *aide
memoire*, the latter will provide photographs to illustrate the review; use
them to draw up the information panel. Double check on basics: times of
opening, telephone number, special offers and so on for the info panel. (See
Figure 24.)

When you and your companion peruse the menu, try to make a wide
choice to give the reader a fuller picture. Even if it is a set menu, it may be
possible to request other items – if afters comprise cheese and biscuits, ask
for a dessert. Chat to the staff behind the car and the ones waiting at table;
a good atmosphere contributes as much to a pleasant evening out as good
food.

Providing feedback – what to do, what not to do

When the waiter quietly asks you if everything is all right, do not nod violently in agreement if this is not the case. Restaurant managers despair of
their customers because they rarely get any feedback; somehow, it's regarded as bad manners to complain: 'Goodness, that mornay sauce is hard
enough to cut with a knife!' 'Hush, darling, please. Don't make a fuss. We
just won't come here again.'

On the other hand, there's no need to storm over to the dessert trolley to
look for extra large custard-pies. Simply mention the problem, very dis-
creetly, *not*: 'My God, I've had tastier school dinners!' If you are tactful in
pointing out anything remiss, any restaurant manager worth his salt will
appreciate it since it means providing customers with a better service and
higher standards, which in turn ensures their loyalty.

Matthew Fort of *The Guardian* claims that 'by and large, restauranteurs
think that critics are a collection of jumped-up, know-nothing parasites . . .'.
However, he did mention in one review that he had once cancelled a reser-
vation because 'when I came to survey the menu outside I was over-
whelmed by *ennui*'. That comment resulted in a thank-you letter some
months later, because the owner had closed down, reorganised everything
(in particular, the menu), and takings had shot up.

WRITING A RESTAURANT REVIEW

The maximum length is usually 500 words. Start by describing the location, the room itself, perhaps some interesting facts about the restaurant and what you've gleaned from the manager or the staff. When it comes to the nitty gritty (and let's hope you never have a meal that bad), try not to describe the food like it's a shopping list. Convey your enjoyment: the delicious aromas, the attractive presentation, the wonderful flavours. Give credit where it's due, compliments to *all* the staff, not just the chef.

The information panel contains the address (with directions if necessary) and telephone number; opening times; amenities (disabled access, beer garden and so on); special offers, specialities or theme nights. Sometimes, especially if done as an advertorial, the manager may be willing to provide meals as a readers' offer or as a competition prize.

CASE STUDIES

Dexter ends up in the soup

Dexter takes his girlfriend to review a new restaurant; he's not that keen on Greek food but it's her favourite. The manager insists on telling them his life-and-hard-times story but finally leaves them in peace to enjoy a romantic candle-lit dinner for two, which Dexter has to eat in between trying to make sense of his notes. When the manager's shift finishes, he goes home, without leaving a message with his assistant who doesn't believe that the meal was complimentary. After a lengthy argument, Dexter has to borrow money from his companion to pay the bill.

Brent goes off course again

Brent is told by the editor that the advertising manager has had a brilliant idea: an article featuring one item from each section: best film and so on. Brent is asked to write about a nearby award-winning museum. Unfortunately, it's not quite near enough as far as he is concerned. Besides, he's been there once, it can't have changed that much, and there's a brochure with enough information to put the piece together. However, the building is due to be closed down for several months for major refurbishment.

Katrina loses her festive spirit

Katrina spends hours on umpteen phone calls, letters and faxes (dealing with somebody different every time) before the organisers of the summer's main festival agree to let her have a press ticket – at the last minute. On the day, everything is badly organised, most of the press ticket holders, instead of getting priority, miss several of the best events through a series of delays. The finished article (a photocopy of which has been promised to the organisers) is combined with a piece by another writer, featuring other festivals, and uses only two short paragraphs from hers.

DISCUSSION POINTS

1. Which leisure activities do you most enjoy?

2. Are you thinking of going into travel writing? Have you got the time – the patience – the money?

3. What about the skills required: motivation and organisation, languages, geography and history? – and photography?

ASSIGNMENT

Draw up a letter of introduction to the manager of a hotel, asking for a press ticket for a special gala evening in aid of charity – and then one of apology when the editor of the publication who commissioned it turns it down 'due to circumstances beyond his control'.

10
Moving On

Reviewing makes an interesting hobby and a fascinating career; it's something which anyone who is interested in writing can have a go at, or make use of to move on to other things. This final chapter therefore, discusses the following:

- other writing opportunities
- what your priorities are
- writing for different markets
- interview techniques and ideas
- other options available to you.

LOOKING AROUND: OTHER WRITING, OTHER MARKETS

So where are you heading? What are your future plans? The great thing about reviews is their versatility:

- You can write them purely as an amateur, indulging your love of the arts.

- You can do it professionally, as part of your job.

- You can use them as a springboard for a career as a writer. Virtually any kind of writing: novels, poetry, journalism, non-fiction.

In a remarkably short space of time, you could go from writing reviews to writing books about writing reviews. Despite many reviews being done in-house, there are still opportunities because of the demand. Besides, experts are sometimes out of touch with newcomers and don't always provide the basic information or communicate the necessary knowledge successfully. If you adopt an empirical approach, learning by experience, that in itself can establish your credentials, especially if you have a knack for being able to pass such information on to others.

Testing the water

To query or not to query? There's no question – you shouldn't ever send any old thing off to the first available magazine. Always start by requesting guidelines; every publication has particular requirements. Enquiry letters should then focus on the following:

- Include two to three article titles, with summaries.

- Suggest a series if you have enough material.

- Mention if photographs are available.

Make sure you note any of the editor's requirements or idiosyncracies – a loathing of brightly coloured paperclips may doom your submissions, which would be a pity if you hoped to become a regular contributor. Start keeping a portfolio of published work, plus a collection of newspaper cuttings on subjects you have covered. These can be added to your original files to update them.

SPECIALISING OR DIVERSIFYING

It is commonly held that the best way to succeed is by concentrating on writing about what you know best and thus carve a niche. To quote John Dawes, chairman of the Author–Publisher Network (A–P N): 'The specialist can do better in freelancing than the generalist.'

Getting to know your likes and dislikes

If you have been writing reviews about most of the arts, you'll know what you prefer to avoid. It could be something you dislike or something you aren't comfortable with because you feel you don't completely understand it. Being a freelance writer doesn't mean you can always please yourself – earning a living often entails doing exactly what you are told. Still, you can usually suit yourself rather more than people who work from nine to five.

The key to successful writing is to enjoy it and to convey that enjoyment so the reader is both entertained and informed. Admittedly, sometimes the very thought of writing a review can seem an insurmountable task. But seeing it there in black and white is always exhilarating.

Finding out what suits you best

Having decided on which area you wish to concentrate, the next thing to consider is the form your writing should take:

- Do you plan to continue writing reviews?

Outstanding performance

by Carole Baldock

Nearly 45 years old, *Stand Magazine* is one of the most venerable literary magazines, yet is still very much in touch with today.

A recent issue contained poetry by Michael Hamburger and Robert Bly (author of *Iron John*), and thought-provoking prose from Celia Bryce and R.N. Friedland. There are also occasional views and literary criticism from Fred Beake, John Lucas and William Scammell.

Editor Jon Silkin says, 'Our word limit on new writing is about 8,000, but we hope that while people may want to write that much, most stories will be between 2,000 and 4,000. We go for fiction, rather than genre – anything that is fresh, inventive and first hand.'

Stand Magazine is also running its first poetry competition offering £2,500 in prizes with publication for the top ten poems. There is a maximum length of 500 lines 'so that entrants can feel free to develop the inner form and the outer structure of their work'. The judges are Denise Riley and Ken Smith and the competition has a closing date of 30 June.

Send sae for subscription details to *Stand* and/or for an entry form for the poetry competition to: **Jon Silkin, Editor, Stand Magazine, 179 Wingrove Road, Newcastle upon Tyne NE4 9DA. Tel/fax: 0191 273 3280.**

Fig. 25. *Writers News* item.

● Does marketing appeal: previews, promotional material?

● Or would you prefer journalistic writing: news items, features, profiles? See Figure 25, the item in *Writers News*.

● Can you utilise the contacts you have made (or even your reviews) to set up interviews?

● What about writing articles, essays or even books?

This last is not so far-fetched, since at some point, you'll have written enough to fill a book. Just as articles on a theme can be collected together and published as a book, so chapters can be adapted as articles. You then sell what you have written at least twice over. Besides, many articles, with some adjustment, can be submitted to a variety of outlets. One piece on youth theatre may interest magazines covering drama, young people, leisure or education.

ADAPTING YOUR STYLE

Another important decision – where do you want to publish your work? In literary publications or popular magazines? – or both? It is possible, if you are able to alter your style:

- formal
- informal
- factual
- metaphorical
- surreal
- iconoclastic

Every publication has its own readership who is used to being addressed in a particular tone, and your work must fit in. Very often, the best opportunities lie with new publications, whose editors are most likely to give new writers a hearing (or a reading). There are some drawbacks with these:

- They will be inundated with freelance submissions.
- They may not be able to pay very high rates.
- Only a few manage to establish themselves.

Researching your markets

You must be very well-acquainted with potential markets – one estimate suggests that only 2 per cent of submissions are 100 per cent suitable. Another claims that more is submitted in a week than gets published in a whole year. Roland John, who edits *Outposts Poetry Quarterly* (the clue is in the title), revealed that in one week, he had received: 'an autobiography, two children's stories, a highly academic article on North American Indians and three novels'.

It's the well thought out, well-researched ideas that match a magazine's particular requirements which stand out above the rest. It may be heretical to say so, but good ideas count for more than good writing. Writing can be improved upon, but a paucity of ideas will have you permanently stumped. Everything has what in marketing terms is known as a 'unique selling factor; if you have a novel idea for Christmas, it'll be an absolute gift to the editor.

Finding something different

When considering the potential of reviews, try to pick an unusual angle – but don't ignore the obvious. If everyone followed this advice, it would be self-defeating – obviously, yet it's startling how it can be overlooked. One idea for an article about the origins of pantomime was initially dismissed because it was assumed to have been done to death. Not so, and the feature has been updated nearly every year and sold to various publications.

Anniversaries feature regularly. Recently, it was the turn of Marilyn Monroe: what would she have been like at 70? What really happened when she died? Could you come up with something completely different? It isn't easy but one way to start would be to look at other events which took place 70 years ago, or what else was going on the year she died.

In the end, successful writing is making your own luck, not hoping to rely on Lady Luck.

Thinking laterally

Some reviews, *per se*, can be hard to place. The most likely possibility is your own column in an arts or literary magazine, covering news, views and reviews. But keep in mind the usefulness of reviews as a means of information and networking – what is required here is some lateral thinking:

Art
A **feature** being considered by an arts magazine: *Art, for God's sake!* What does the man in the street (or the woman in the gallery) make of art today?

Music
An **article** about the Royal Liverpool Philharmonic Society (RLPS) for leisure interest and/or youth market: *Brahms and Liszt*: and what else does the RLPS have to offer?

Leisure
A **review** of RLPS restaurant – possibility of regular series: *Ladies who lunch.*

Performance
A **feature** for general interest title: *But seriously now, folks . . .* Comedians who want to do straight acting.

Film and Video
Books reviews expanded to include film and video in a double page spread.

Literature
A **book review** incorporated in a news item, leading to regular contributions of the latter.

DEVELOPING REVIEWS INTO INTERVIEWS

Different publications look at different angles:

EDDIE IZZARD

TV OR NOT TV?

by Carole Baldock

Single-minded? You could say that. A person who values his independence, Eddie Izzard has always gone his own way. Funny peculiar or funny haha, the man voted Britain's best stand up comedian is far more interested in frocks than the box.

Eddie Izzard was born in Yemen in 1962, where his father worked for BP; his mother was a nurse at the refinery hospital. Two years later, they moved to Northern Ireland, then on to Skewen in 1967: "Had a rough time in Wales, essentially due to mum dying in '68. Before she died, she and dad decided that the best way for the family to continue was for me and big brother to go off to boarding schools. It was 12 years. "It made me very independently minded, but also emotionally dead". Aged six, he went to St John's in Portcawl: "It was run by Mr Crump - 'the man from hell who we hate. 'Seeing as my mum had just died I decided to cry relentlessly for a year. Mr Crump would help me along with beatings when he could fit them in."

Fortunately in 1969, the Izzards moved yet again, this time to Eastbourne; when seven year old Eddie saw a play in the school gym, he knew that he had to be a professional performer. As for being a transvestite. . .

"It's like a passion for chocolate," is Eddie's description, "You're longing for something which is forbidden, AND all around you, everybody is tucking in. 'It was so hard, keeping quiet. I agonised for a year, and it took every ounce of courage to come out, but I should have done it much sooner. And I'd repressed it for so long, it was that teen-age girl thing, you know, hitting the bloody wall, all over the place." Clothes can be a problem, working out what suits you when you can't go into a shop and try them on. You just have to get them from a catalogue, then it's trial and error."

He has become very relaxed at this point; we even swapped a few tips, hands held out,

comparing nail varnish. Don't most people automatically assume that a transvestite must be gay? "That doesn't bother me at all, though I'm not. If I were a woman I'd be a lesbian." he assures me, adding, "I don't know how come I'm not bisexual." He sounds almost regretful, I comment, but he just shrugs, as if he's puzzled, and goes on: "Transvestites have always been around, it just isn't generally acknowledged. Look at Marlene Dietrich in the 20s. But it isn't a fantasy thing for me, he emphasises, "It's more ordinary, more everyday."

And sometimes, you have to be VERY determined - do men in skirts look daft because we're not used to seeing them dressed like that, I ask, tactless again, or because they just look daft? "Some men have very nice legs." Eddie reminds me about kilts, "I think I'm probably going to settle for leggings and skirts," he tells me. If you're on TV, you have to learn how to walk, how to sit, how to behave as a woman. And there's so much more to think about. You no longer have that freedom of choice. You have to anticipate other people's reactions; they can be aggressive, hostile. It's not just a question of wearing female clothes, you're putting on female characteristics too. Straightaway, you're weaker, you're seen as being more vulnerable. Men who prize strength , they've grown up to think so much more of physical strength. They're just meatheads." he concludes contemptuously.

Fig. 26. Eddie Izzard interview.

106

- **family magazines:** celebrity childhood (see Figure 26 for an example of an interview)
- **women's magazines:** relationships; health matters
- **specialist magazines:** favourite hobbies
- **writing magazines:** how to become rich and famous

Choosing your questions

If interviews don't appeal to you because it's hard work finding out all that information, remember that you've probably already had some experience researching for articles, which usually involves asking a few questions. Most press packs provide enough information to inspire you.

Many publications include a celebrity questionnaire and they're remarkably similar. If you were a celebrity, what would you like to talk about? Try drawing up a sample questionnaire as it can be useful to submit this in advance and there's more likelihood of in-depth replies:

- What made you first think of doing this?

- What would you say was your 'first lucky break'?

- What are your future plans?

- Who have been your main influences?

- How would your best friend describe you in one sentence?

It can be complicated setting up an interview and it may take you ages. Plus, if you are overawed at the idea of finally meeting your hero . . . well, sometimes you'll have the time of your life, sometimes you'll come away sadly disillusioned.

Nevertheless, be professional, and properly prepared:

- Study the press pack from cover to cover.

- Read the latest book; watch the latest film, video *etc.*

- Make sure you are properly organised.

- Allow plenty of time to get to the meeting and for the meeting to take place.

- Also allow yourself time to write the interview up and send it off well before the deadline.

HOPELESS CASES?

Are you sick to death of rejection slips?

Are you fed up trying to work out why you can't get your work published?

Does your friend keep warning you never to give up the day job?

Does your mother keep asking when you're going to get a proper job?

GOOD NEWS!!!

WE'VE done ALL the hard work so YOU can take it easy:

Send £250 with your short story mss or poem (maximum 20 lines please) for an in-depth analysis, specially tailored for ALL your needs to:

Hopeless Cases, c/o 52 Dorrell Park, London SE19 6XJ.

NO TIMEWASTERS PLEASE

Fig. 27. An advertisement for a critique.

Double-check everything you are taking with you:

- notebook and notes
- spare pen
- dictaphone and spare batteries
- camera (and that you know how to work it)

UTILISING REVIEWS FOR APPRAISAL AND INFORMATION

Other areas where writing reviews forms a solid foundation are:

- providing critiques
- operating an appraisal service
- providing information services.

Many writing competitions offer optional critiques for a slightly higher entry fee. The demand seems to have arisen because new writers often complain that editors never give sufficient reasons for rejection. Writing magazines and writers' organisations and societies often include an appraisal service for members. These can be expensive but the critique is likely to be in-depth; competitions usually restrict themselves to providing a checklist, highlighting the weaknesses and strengths. Figure 27 is an advertisement for a critique.

There is little difference between a review and a critique; both call upon similar skills. A critique, done on a one-to-one basis, is more personal and the words 'constructive criticism' should be kept in mind. After all, to unearth hidden talent and help that person become successful is nearly as gratifying as your own success.

Freelancing can be far from easy but most contacts lead on to something else, often even more interesting, prestigious *and* lucrative. So you could consider running an information service, especially if people are always getting in touch to ask your advice. It is far easier to find things out by talking to somebody than to wander around a library.

Keeping ahead of the game

Writing reviews means you will have plenty of useful contacts; it's astonishing how often the left hand hasn't even noticed that there is a right hand. Logically, editors of a literary magazine might be assumed to know about every other literary magazine, because they need to keep an eye on the opposition and this keep ahead of the game when the name of the game is survival. But editors are very busy people.

You, on the other hand, by the symbotic nature of reviewing, are perhaps more closely connected with the network. Place a review with one

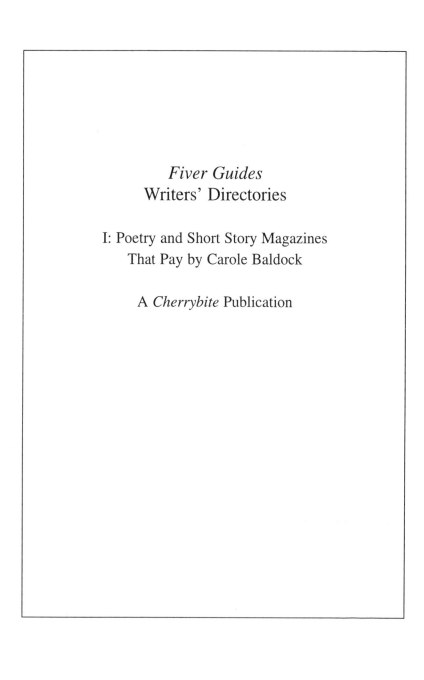

Fiver Guides
Writers' Directories

I: Poetry and Short Story Magazines
That Pay by Carole Baldock

A *Cherrybite* Publication

Fig. 28. Example of a directory cover.

magazine and you have established two outlets and can expect more work from the originator as well as the destination; as the outlets increase, eventually, the result is synergy, *ie* 1 + 1 = 3.

Besides, if you don't know the answer to something, you almost certainly know somebody who does. By the time you have acquired a long list of names and addresses, it is well worth considering compiling it into a directory or selling it as a booklet. Information is a valuable commodity. See Figure 28.

CASE STUDIES

Dexter has the last laugh

Dexter has sent some of his best gags off to Dolly Daydream but has had no reply. Every time he rings the portable phone number he's been given it always seems to be when the comic is rushing for a train or busy rehearsing. Then Dexter gets a call from Dolly's agent to explain that they're off on a world tour. So that's that. Well, not quite. There's been a couple of double bookings in the city so the agent arranges for Dexter to stand in for Dolly, and make his debut doing his own stand up routine.

Brent goes completely off the rails

Brent has received a fax from the recording company. They are quite impressed with the demo and would like him and *Qute* to come down to audition in London. But it's very short notice and with all the running round and making and changing arrangements, tempers are short. At the station, a frank and open discussion about the song they should perform degenerates into a row. Brent and the keyboard player come to blows, wrecking the drum kit in the process; the drummer storm off in a huff. *Qute* finally split up for good.

Katrina comes up with a sort of novel idea

Katrina has been asked by the editor to organise the competition prizes and reader's offers; the advertising manager has quite enough to do. Reluctantly, she starts to get in touch with some publishers; with summer coming up, books for tourists should be popular. She notices that one catalogue covers the whole of the country, except there is very little about the area where she lives. She rings backs and after a long conversation, they ask her to send in her CV and some cuttings, with a view to writing a book.

DISCUSSION POINTS

1. What kind of writing do you enjoy most: creative, non-fiction, journalistic *etc*?

2. Which forms of writing are your strong points: fillers, articles, interviews, books?

3. Have you considered trying your hand at marketing, critiques or information provision?

ASSIGNMENT

Turn one of your reviews into a preview

(a) for a student magazine

(b) for a literary publication.

Glossary

Advertorial. A feature particularly in the local press, incorporating one or more advertisements, focusing on a particular shop or business, sometimes covering several, such as companies specialising in weekend breaks.

Article. An item of prose on one particular subject or a group of related themes; can range in length from 500 – 2500 words. See also feature.

Backlist. Books still in print, *ie* not the latest publications.

Blurb. A piece of writing, invariably somewhat over-the-top since it is used for promotion, usually on the back of books; can apply to flyers and press releases.

Book launch. Well-publicised event (in theory) starring the author, to attract press and audience in order to promote and sell a new publication.

Bullet. Also, stab point. Large dot at the beginning of a line to emphasise items, particularly those in lists.

By-line. Identifies the author of a particular piece of writing, appearing either as part of the heading or at the end. It is quite unusual for magazines not to use them but some tuck them away in the margin.

Complimentary copy (Voucher copy). Sent to a writer as a courtesy, being an issue in which their work has appeared, also as evidence *ie* vouching that the work has been published.

Conference. See seminar.

Copy. The prepared typescript submitted for publication, prior to being typeset.

Copyright. In law, the exclusive right of an author or other designated party, or an original piece of work.

Copywriting. Material which is written for promotional purposes: advertising, publicity and so on.

Deadline. Every writer's (and editor's) worst nightmare: the final date by which the work must be handed in.

Distributor. Company which sends out books, records, videos and so on to the various retail outlets throughout the country.

Draft. The initial or kitchen sink version of a piece of work.

FBSR. First British Serial Rights *ie* to publish a story or article for the first time and once only in the UK. Where articles are concerned, they can later be revised and updated then offered to another publication.

Feature. See article, the two words being virtually synonymous; a one-off piece for a magazine or newspaper.

Filler. Item of limited length (usually general knowledge), used to 'fill' gaps in magazine layout; payment can be quite lucrative.

Flyer. Promotional leaflet, often distributed via the post or inside other publications.

Freebie. Slang term for a freesheet but more commonly anything given away free, particularly readers offers; sometimes incorrectly used for review copies, press tickets, invitations and so on.

Freelance. Self-employed writer or journalist who sells work to various publications.

Genre. One specific category of writing or area of literature such as horror writing or romance.

Gig. Rock or popular music concert, booking for a band in a small scale venue *eg* a pub.

Guidelines. Set of instructions drawn up by a publication regarding their requirements, the various **dos** and **dont's**, to assist would-be contributors.

Independent press. More commonly known as 'the small press', though this term is becoming more popular, especially as it avoids derogatory connotations.

In-house. Copy written by staff-writers, people working in the offices of a publication.

ISBN. International Standard Book Number, the unique reference number identifying every book which is published.

ISSN. International Standard Series Number – as above, allocated to periodical publications.

Journalist. Somebody who writes for a newspaper, magazine, journal, as opposed to writing a book.

Layout. The appearance of the printed page.

Libel. A malicious or defamatory statement which has been printed or broadcast. Sometimes confused with slander, which is spoken (or by looks, signs or gestures).

Ligging. Getting things for nothing, particularly in the music business.

Mailing List. Database maintained by organisations containing names and addresses to ensure press releases are automatically sent out.

Mainstream. Traditional or current subjects, notably in literature, as opposed to category, genre or 'slipstream'.

Market research. In depth study of possible publication outlets. Vital for all writers.

Media. TV, radio, publications as a means of communication and sources of information.

Negotiable. Term frequently employed for rates of payment, usually taken at face value by contributors, especially when first approaching a publication – but there's no harm in asking. Equally uninformative is the term 'usual rates' – how do you know what the other contributors are 'usually paid'?

Networking. Building up contacts; an informal collection of people committed to helping one another and thus helping themselves – invaluable for a freelance as each collaboration often leads to another.

On spec. (*ie* speculation). Work which an editor suggests you submit but without guarantee of acceptance. Also, work which you have submitted which has not previously been commissioned or invited. See also unsolicited submission.

Outline. A proposal for a piece of work, stating its purpose and containing very brief details of the areas to be covered.

Plagiarism. Reproducing part of somebody else's work without their permission. Invariably claimed to have been done accidentally.

Press call. Advance notification; invitation to reviewers to promote a forthcoming event: a concert or a play, a theatre company debut or the opening of a new tourist attraction.

Press launch. Promotes an imminent event. A press lunch, of course, usually means visiting a new restaurant.

Press night. The evening for which invitations are issued to the media to attend a play, a block of seats being reserved in advance; usually the second or third night, giving cast and director a chance to resolve any last minute problems.

Press pack. Issued to reviewers to provide background information about new films, performances and so on. Often includes photographs.

Press release. Promotional material issued to the media.

Press show or preview. Private showing of a film prior to general release.

Private view. Invitation to see a new exhibition before it is opened to the public.

Professional journal. A publication relating to a specific profession: *Publishing News* has a readership of writers. Similarly, trade journal.

Programme. Brochure issued at a play or a concert. Also, the list of events which will take place at a particular venue.

Proofs. A typeset copy of your original typescript returned for checking before being printed.

Readership. Those who regularly subscribe to or purchase a particular publication.

Seminar. Usually a class for a group of students and their tutor, also virtually synonymous with conference – a discussion group, often on a large scale. The event may also include guest speakers and workshops.

Showcase. A performance in brief, to demonstrate skills acquired at a workshop or on a course; also used as a fore-taster at a press call, to encourage reviewers to visit an event.

Small press. See Independent Press

Staff-writer. See In-house.

Submission. Any work forwarded to a publisher or an editor, with a view to publication.

Text. The typeset matter in a book, exclusive of headings, illustrations and so on.

Trade journal. See professional journal.

Unsolicited submission. A phrase commonly used by publications to deter would-be contributors from submitting articles, short stories and so on. Often misunderstood to mean 'don't come near us', but in fact, you can sometimes approach the features editor with an idea, providing you stick strictly to the outline. See also on-spec.

Usual rates/terms. See under negotiable.

Workshop. A group of people under the guidance of a leader who meet to discuss work in progress, as opposed to a writers' circle or group, where the work will already have been completed.

Further Reading

GENERAL WRITING AND JOURNALISTIC SKILLS

Books

Becoming a Writer, by Dorothea Brande, (Macmillan, 1996). Originally published in 1934, Malcolm Bradbury's introduction refers to it as a 'living classic'.

The Craft of Writing Articles, by Gordon Wells (Allison & Busby, 1983).

Creative Conversations: The Writer's Guild to Conducting Interviews, by Michael Schumacher (Writer's Digest Books, 1991).

Freelance Writing for Newspapers, by Jill Dick (A. & C. Black, 1991.

Getting to grips with Writing, by Catherine Hilton and Margaret Hyder (Letts Educational, 1995). Other titles cover punctuation and grammar, spelling, vocabulary.

How to Be a Freelance Journalist, Christine Hall (How To Books, 1996).

How to Write for Publication, by Chriss McCallum (How To Books, 3rd edition, 1995).

The Magazine Writer's Handbook, by Gordon Wells (Allison & Busby, 1994).

Starting to Write, by Marina and Deborah Oliver (How To Books, 1996).

The Writer's Companion, by Barry Turner (Macmillan, 1996).

Writer's Questions Answered, by Gordon Wells (Allison & Busby, 1986).

Writing Feature Articles, by Brendan Hennessy (Heinemann Professional Publishing, 1989).

Writing for Magazines, by Jill Dick (A & C Black, 1994).

Magazines

British Journalism Review (q), editor Geoffrey Goodman. Subs £25 pa. John Libby Media, Faculty of Humanities, University of Luton, 75 Castle Street, Luton, Bedfordshire, LU1 3AJ.

Publishing News (w), editor Rodney Burbeck. £1.70. 43 Museum Street, London, WC1A 1LY.

Reference books

NB You can always consult these in the library, but those marked * are essential buys.

BRAD (British Rates and Data), EMAP, monthly pb. £150. Useful source for market research, listing consumer and business publications, with brief editorial profile
**Chambers Dictionary* (Chambers, 1994).
Research for Writers, Ann Hoffman (A. & C. Black, 1994).
**Roget's Thesaurus,* pocket version (Longman, 1995).
Willings Press Guide (IPC Business Press, annual). Similar to *BRAD.*
Writers' & Artists' Yearbook, (A. & C. Black, annual).
The Writer's Handbook, edited by Barry Turner (Macmillan/Pen, annual).
*NB either of the last two are an essential buy.

Writing magazines

ALWAYS enclose SAE; *b* = bi-monthly, *m* = monthly; *q* = quarterly.
The New Writer (merger between Quartos and Acclaim; 10 issues pa) editor, Suzanne Ruthven. PO Box 60, Cranbrook, Kent TN17 2ZR.
Writers' Forum (q): editor, John Benton. £14.50 pa. 9/10 Roberts Close, Moxley, Wednesday, West Midlands, WS10 8SS.
Writers' Monthly (m): editor, Alan Williams. £33.50 pa. 29 Turnpike Lane, London N8 0EP. Tel: (0181) 342 8879. Fax: (0181) 347 8847.
Writers News (m; plus *Writing Magazine b),* editor Richard Bell. £41.60 pa. Writers News Limited, PO Box 4, Nairn IV12 4HU.

REVIEWING SKILLS AND LITERARY THEORY

Approaching Literature: An Introduction to Literary Criticism by Sue Collins (Hodder & Stoughton, 1992). An excellent book to start off with, covering the novel, poetry and the theatre. This Teach Yourself series also includes *Creative Writing* by Dianne Doubtfire (1996).
How To Begin Studying English Literature, by Nicholas Marsh (Macmillan, 1995).
How To Study Modern Drama by Kenneth Pickering (Macmillan, 1988).
How To Study Modern Poetry by Tony Curtis (Macmillan, 1993). There is a long list of titles in this *How To Study* series by Macmillan, many of which deal with specific authors.
Literature in the Modern World, edited by Dennis Walder (Oxford University Press, 1990).
Modern Criticism and Theory, edited by David Lodge (Longman, 1995).
The Novel, by Andrew Michael Robers (Bloomsbury, 1994).
Practical Criticism by John Peck and Martin Coyle (Macmillan, 1995).
Victorian Literature, 1830–1900, edited by Jane Thomas (Bloomsbury, 1994).
York Notes published by Longman cover a wide range of literary titles and are suitable for GCSE level or university. They are good value and provide biographical, literary and historical background to texts.

LITERATURE

Books
See above.

Magazines
Bibliophile, editor Anne Quigley. Lists bargain and secondhand books. No charge. 5 Thomas Road, London E14 7BN.

Book & Magazine Collector (m), editor Crispin Jackson. £2.30. 43–45 St Mary's Road, Ealing, London W5 5RQ.

Bookseller, editor Louis Baum. £1.95 per weekly issue. 12 Dyott Street, London WC1A 1DF. Tel: (0171) 836 8911; fax: (0171) 836 6381.

Books in The Media. £103 pa; weekly issues. Peter Harland, Director & Publisher, Bookwatch Ltd, 15-Up East Street, Lewin's Yard, Chesham, Bucks HP5 1HQ. Tel: (01494) 792269; fax: (01494) 784850.

Books Magazines (b), editor Liz Thomson. Free from bookshops. 43, Museum Street, London WC1 1LY. Tel: (0171) 404 0304.

ART

Books
The Penguin Dictionary of Art and Artists, by Peter and Linda Murray (Penguin, 1995) pb, £5.99.

Understanding Modern Art, by Monica Bohm-Duchen and Janet Cook (Usborne, 1991).

The Story of Art, by E. H. Gombrich. (Phaidon, 1995).

Magazines
Art Monthly, editor Patricia Bickers. £2.75. Suite 17, 26 Charing Cross Road, London WC2H 0DG. Tel/Fax: (0171) 240 0389.

tate The art magazine, available 3 times a year from the eponymous galleries and selected outlets £2.95 an issue. NB although it 'reflects the expanding role of the gallery in the contemporary cultural debate, it is an independent publication with its own voice and vision'. Well worth perusing. Blueprint Media Ltd, Christ Church, Cosway Street, London NW1 5NJ.

MUSIC

Books
Pandora Guide to Women Composers: Britain and the United States 1629–Present, by Sophie Fuller (Pandora, 1994).

Understanding Music, by Judy Tatchell (Usborne, 1992).

Virgin Guide to Classical Music, by Jeremy J. Beadle (Virgin, 1993).

Women, Sex and Rock 'n' Roll: In their own words, by Liz Evans (Pandora, 1994).

Magazines available on news stands
Classic CD; Classic FM; Classical Music; Empire; Kerrang; Premier; Raw; Select; Sight & Sound; Smash Hits; Vox for rock and pop music.

PERFORMANCE

Books
Acting and Theatre, by Cheryl Evans and Lucy Smith (Usborne, 1992).
Oxford Illustrated History of Theatre, edited by John Russell Brown, Oxford University Press.

Magazines
Plays and Players (m): editor, Sandra Rennie. £2.50. Mineco Design Ltd, Northway House, 1379 High Road, London N20 9LP. Tel: (0181) 343 8515; fax: (0181) 446 1410.
The Stage (incorporating *Television Today) (w),* 80p. Peter Hepple, Reviews Editor, The Stage, Stage House, 47 Bermondsey Street, London SE1 3XT.
Theatre Magazine (b): editor, Ann Shuttleworth; £2.00. 67 Eastwell Street, Weston Street, London SE1 4DJ. Tel: (0171) 378 1055; fax: (0171) 378 1069.
Theatre Record (f) editor Ian Herbert, £4. 4 Cross Deep Gardens, Twickenham, Middlesex TW1 4QU. Tel: (0181) 892 6087; fax: (0181) 744 3002.

FILM AND VIDEO

Books
Halliwells's Film Guide, edited by John Walker (HarperCollins, 10th edition 1995).
Videohound Golden Movie Retriever; Videohound and AMG All-Movie Guide 'Stargazer' (Visible Ink Press, 1996).

Magazines available on news stands
Empire; Premiere; Sight and Sound.

LEISURE

Books
A Guide to Travel Writing and Photography, by Ann and Carl Purcell (Writer's Digest Books, 1991).

How To Write Travel Articles, by Cathy Smith (Allison & Busby, 1992).
Writing About Travel, by Morag Campbell (A. & C. Black, 1989).

Magazines

Between The Lines, Livewire and so on. The Intercity Magazine Group Distribution for travellers using the various rail services. The Illustrated London News Group, 20 Upper Ground, London SE1 9PF.

Freetime (q), editor Julian Dresser. free magazine issued to regional railways passengers. Freetime Publications UK Limited, 117 Northenden Road, Sale Moor, Cheshire M33 3HF.

Skylines (b), managing editor, Valerie Cottle. Free in-flight magazine of British Airways Express. Mannin Media Group, Spring Valley Industrial Estate, Douglas, Isle of Man IM2 2QT.

Travel Trade Gazette (w), deputy editor Howard Carr. Miller Freeman Travel Group, Miller Freeman Technical Ltd, 30 Calderwood Street, London SE18 6QH.

SMALL INDEPENDENT PRESS PUBLICATIONS

Please note that when contacting magazines, *always* send a SAE.

Useful sources of marketing information

Booklets and packs

Back Brain Recluse (BBR), published by the New SF Alliance (NSFA), includes a directory of over 160 outlets, reviews, letters, articles and stories. Subs for four issues: £11; single copy £3.50.

Fiver Guides, A series of writers' directories. *I: Poetry and Short Story Magazines that Pay,* by Carole Baldock. Covers over 30 outlets, including some taking reviews. In preparation – *II: Essential Reading and Networking.* £5 a copy. Cherrybite Publications, Linden Cottage, 45 Burton Road, Little Neston, South Wirral L64 4AE.

Flomona Press, and information pack 'in support of the Independent/ Small Press'. Contact with SAE and two stamps: Harry D. Crossley, Flomona Press, River Court, Strang Road, Union Mills, Isle of Man IM4 4NN.

Light's List, annual booklet (£1) covering the Small/Independent Presses. John Light, Photon Press, 29 Longfield Road, Tring, Herts HP23 4DG.

Scavenger's Newsletter, a monthly publication with listings, articles, letters and reviews. Subs £18 pa. Chris Reed, BBR Distribution, PO Box 625, Sheffield S1 3GY.

Magazines

Cambrensis (q): editor, Arthur Smith. A magazine for writers born or resident in Wales, or with some Welsh connection. Includes four page listings, *The Zine Scene*. £6 pa. 41 Heol Fach, Cornelly, Bridgend CF33 4LN.

Freelance Market News, see under Useful Addresses: The Association of Freelance Writers.

Lateral Moves (q), editor, Alan White. £1.50 per issue. Aural Images, 5 Hamilton Street, Astley Bridge, Bolton BL1 6RJ.

New Hope International (b), editor, Gerald England. £15 pa: magazine, chapbooks and annual booklet, *The Review* (single copy £3), which covers lots of Small Press magazines, as well as books, software, cassettes, CDs and so on. 20 Werneth Avenue, Gee Cross, Hyde, Cheshire SK14 5NL.

Writers' Guide (b), editor, G. Carroll. £10 pa, £1.80 single issue. 11 Shirley Street, Hove, East Sussex BN3 3WJ.

Writers' Update (q), editor, Richard P. D. Williams. Electronic magazine, shortly available on the Internet. £14.95 pa, including free software: send for sample disk and you can return it at no charge, keep it on payment of £2.50 (saving more than £1.20 on the usual single-issue price) or subscribe for the next four issues within 10 days and keep the disk as well as receiving a free software guide. Contact: Way Ahead, 27 Woodford Green, Bratton, Telford, Shropshire TF5 0NS. Tel/fax: (01952) 243153. E-mail: wayahead@cix.compulink.co.uk or Internet: hhttp://www/demon.co.uk/hsc/wayahead

Zene: The Guide to the Independent Press (q), editor, Andy Cox. £7 pa, sample issue £1.95. 5 Martins Lane, Witcham, Ely, Cambs CB6 2LB.

Magazines with a review section

(b = bi-monthly, m = monthly; q = quarterly; t = twice-yearly; tt = three times a year; w = weekly. NB e = erratic, or rather, 'even more problems with funding').

Acumen (tt), editor, Patricia Oxley. £10 pa, single issue £3.45. Poetry, short stories, essays, translations, interviews, reviews. 6 The Mount, Higher Furzeham, Brixham, South Devon TQ5 8QY.

Agenda (q), editors William Cookson and Peter Dale. £20 pa Poetry, essays, interviews and reviews. 5 Cranbourne Court, Albert Bridge Road, London SW11 4PE.

Ambit (q), editor, Martin Bax. £22 pa; single issue £5.50. Poetry, short stories, essays, reviews, illustrations. FREEPOST, London N6 5BR.

. . . the buzz . . . (m ex August and December), editor, Robin Thornber. £25 pa. Covers all the Arts outside London. Moorfield Lodge, Glossop, Derbyshire SK13 9PP.

Chapman *(q)*, editor, Joy Hendry. £13 pa, single issue £3.45. 'The best in

Scottish writing' – reviews and critical essays. 4 Broughton Place, Edinburgh EH1 3RX.

Critical Quarterly (q), editor, Colin MacCabe. £31 pa. Publishes fiction, poetry, criticism, interviews, reviews. NB only submissions of poetry and short stories required. The British Film Institute, c/o The London Consortium, 21 Stephen Street, London W1P 1PL.

Defying Gravity (b), editor Craig Turner. £10 pa; single copy £2. Publishes poetry, prose, arts reviews. Gravity Publications, 60 Howard Close, Cambridge CB5 8QU.

Envoi (tt), editor, Roger Elkin. £12 pa, back copy £4 and sample copy £3. Poems, articles and reviews. 44 Rudyard Road, Biddulph Manor, Stoke on Trent ST8 7JN.

Essays in Criticism (q), editors, Stephen Wall and Christopher Ricks, £30; single issue £13. Stephen Wall, 6a Rawlinson Road, Oxford OX2 6UE.

The Good Society Review (t), editors, Mary MacGregor and Douglas Brown. £10 pa. Articles, reviews, poetry and prose relating to 'the arts, environment and society'. Holman's Press, Elm Lodge, Union Place, Anstruther Easter, Fife KY10 3HQ. Tel: (01333) 310313.

iota (b), editor, David Holliday. £6 pa, single issue £1.50. Poetry, reviews – lists books and magazines received. 67 Hady Crescent, Chesterfield, Derbyshire S41 0EB.

IRON (q), editor, Peter Mortimer. £12 pa, single issue £3.50. Poetry, short stories, reviews. 5 Marden Terrace, Cullercoats, North Shields, Northumberland NE30 4PD.

London Magazine (b), editor, Alan Ross. £28.50 pa, single issue £5.99. Art, reviews, travel, essays, poetry, prose. 30 Thurloe Place, London SW7 2HQ.

The North (t), editors, Peter Sansom and Janet Fisher. £10 pa; single issue £5.50. Critical articles, reviews, poetry and occasional fiction. The Studio. Byram Arcade, Westgate, Huddersfield HD1 1ND. Tel: (01484) 434840; fax: (01484) 426566.

Orbis (tt), editor, Mike Shields. £15 pa for three issues. Poetry, reviews and listings. The Long Shoot, Nuneaton, Warks CV11 6JQ.

Poetry Life (tt), editor, Adrian Bishop. Subs £6 pa. Poetry, articles, reviews. 14 Pennington Oval, Lymington, Hampshire SO41 8BQ.

The Printer's Devil, editorial board. £15 for three copies. Reviews, articles, prose and poetry. Top Offices, 13A Western Road, Hove, East Sussex BN3 1AE. Tel: (01273) 208739.

the source (b), editors, Corene Lemaître, Andrew Kelly. £16 pa. Poetry, short stories, articles, reviews and illustrations. Lemaître Kelly Publishing, 19 Cumberland Street, Edinburgh EH3 6RT.

Stand (q), editor, Jon Silkin. £10.95, back copies available at 50p. Poetry, short stories, reviews. 179 Wingrove Road, Newcastle upon Tyne, NE4 9DA.

Stride (e), editor Rupert Loydell. £3.95 per issue – 'an occasional arts magazine'. Poetry, short stories, reviews. 11 Sylvan Road, Exeter, Devon EX4 6EW.

Sunk Island Review (t), editor, Michael Blackburn. Essays, £10 pa. Poetry, prose, reviews, articles on cultural issues. PO Box 74, Lincoln LN1 1QG.

Tears in the Fence (e), editor, David Caddy. £7.50 pa for three issues, single issue £2.90. Poetry, stories, reviews, articles and essays; incorporates *Open Press*, which provides news about the Independent Press, usually magazine listings and some book reviews. This was originally a supplement to *Vigil*, edited by John Howard-Graves (12 Priory Mead, Bruton, Somerset BA10 0DZ). 38 Hod View, Stourpaine, Blandford Forum, Dorset CT11 8TN.

Writing Women (e), £3 per issue. Poetry, short stories and reviews. Subscribers include writers such as Helen Dunmore. The Editors, Unit 14, Hawthorn House, Forth Bank, Newcastle upon Tyne, NE1 3SG.

Useful Addresses

ORGANISATIONS AND SOCIETIES

ALP (Association of Little Presses), £12.50 pa: *Palpi (Poetry And Little Press Information*, a twice yearly booklet), a quarterly newsletter and the current catalogue of *Little Press Books in Print*. Co-ordinator: Stan Trevor, 30 Greenhill, Hampstead High Street, London NW3 5UA. Tel: (0171) 435 1889.

A–PN (Author–Publisher Network), £12 pa: shared marketing and joint distribution arrangements, seminars, workshops, bookfairs and promotional events. Also, newsletters, guidelines and reviews, directories and contacts; publications include *Small Publishers A–Z: The Guide to Good Publishing*, by Daphne Macara. Press Officer: John Beasley, South Riding, 6 Everthorpe Road, London SE15 4DA.

British Amateur Press Association, £5 pa: journalism as a hobby. Michaelmas, Cimarron Close, South Woodham Ferrers, Essex CM3 5PB.

The Friends of the Arvon Foundation, £5 pa: regular newsletter – markets, literature, competitions, events and courses. Joan Thornton, 6 Church Street, Darfield, Yorkshire S73 9LG. Tel: (01422) 843714.

The National Small Press Centre, £12 pa: six issues of *News from the Centre*, four of *Small Press Listings*. Open Tues and Thurs, 12–3pm; 24 hours answerphone). Cecilia Boggis (Publicity), c/o Middlesex University, Tottenham Campus, White Hart Lane, London N17 8HR. Tel: (0181) 362 6058.

The Poetry Society, London £27.50 pa, elsewhere £15. Wide range of benefits for members including *Poetry Review Quarterly* and information bulletin, reduced rates for use of critical service. 22 Betterton Street, London WC2H 9BU. Tel: (0171) 250 4810; Fax: (0171) 240 4818.

PROFESSIONAL ASSOCIATIONS

The Arts Council of Great Britain, 14 Great Peter Street, London SW1P 3NQ. Tel: (0171) 333 0100, Fax: (0171) 973 6590.

The Society of Authors, £70 pa: wide range of services, including a free quarterly magazine of approximately 100 pages; *The Author* is edited by Derek Parker and available to non-members at £6 per issue. 84 Drayton Gardens, London SW10 9SB. Tel: (0171) 373 6642, Fax: (0171) 373 5768.

The Society of Women Writers and Journalists, London £25 pa, regional £21: variety of services (manuscript advice, weekend schools, meetings, outings, events, competitions, newsletter). New writers may apply as probationers (maximum number 25). Hon. Membership Secretary, Joyce Elsden, Nash Manor, Horsham Road, Steyning, W. Sussex BN4 3AA.

Women Writers Network, £25 pa: services as for SWWJ, entry above. Membership Secretary, Cathy Smith, 23 Prospect Road, London NW2 2JU. Tel: (0171) 794 5861.

Workers Educational Association (WEA), National Office, Temple House, 9 Upper Berkley Street, London W1H 8BY. Tel: (0181) 983 1515; (0181) 983 4840.

The Writers' Guild of Great Britain. Official magazine, *The Writers' Newsletters* (10 issues pa), edited by Patrick Campbell, available to non-members on subscription. Contact for details of membership rates: 430 Edgware Road, London W2 1EH. Tel: (0171) 723 8074.

SERVICES

The Association of Freelance Writers, £29 pa: services include appraisals, competitions, 11 issues of 16 page newsletter: *Freelance Market News*. Angela Cox, Secretary, The Writers Bureau Ltd, Sevendale House, 7 Dale Street, Manchester M1 1JB. Tel: (0161) 228 2362, Fax: (0161) 228 3533.

Book Trust, excellent literary source: readings, exhibitions, publications, prizes. Send SAE for more details to: The Publicity Officer, Book Trust, Book House, 45 East Hill, London SW18 2QZ. Tel: (0181) 870 9055/8, Fax: (0181) 874 4790.

The Capricorn International Authors' Guild, £35 pa: services include professional criticism and guidance, competitions and newsletter. DG. Tutton, West Lead Road, Bath BA1 3RL.

Flair for Words, £7.50 pa, includes discounts on all products and events: wide variety of services (appraisal and advisory service, newsletter, audio tapes). Sample copy of newsletter: £1. Run by Cass and Janie Jackson, 5 Delavall Walk, Eastbourne, BN23 6ER.

Oriel (Welsh Arts Council's Bookshop), offers services to writers and small/independent press. Peter Finch, Oriel Bookshop, The Friary, Cardiff CF1 4AA. Tel: (01222) 395548.

Real Writers correspondence course, provides appraisal services for members. Registration fee: £10; fee for monthly assignment: £15. Send SAE

for details: Real Writers, PO Box 170, Chesterfield, Derbyshire S40
1FE.

The Writers Advice Centre, critiques (£20 for a short story or article),
workshops, talks, courses, writers' holidays. Run by Nancy Smith, Jane
Baker and Louise Jordan. Send SAE for details: Jane Baker, 6 Bramble
Way, Send Marsh, Woking, Surrey GU23 6LL. Tel: (01483) 223860.

PUBLISHERS OF BOOKS COVERING THE ARTS

Faber and Faber Ltd, 3 Queen Square, London WC1N 3AU. Tel: (0171)
465 0045. Fax: (0171) 465 0034.

Methuen, Michelin House, 81 Fulham Road, London SW3 6RB. Tel:
(0171) 581 9393. Fax: (0171) 225 9424.

Phaidon Press Ltd, 2 Kensington Square, London W8 5EZ (NB art only).
Tel: (0171) 361 1000; Fax: (0171) 361 1010.

Routledge, 11 New Fetter Lane, London EC4P 4EE. Tel: (0171) 583 9855.
Fax: (0171) 842 2298.

Thames and Hudson, 30–34 Bloomsbury Street, London WC1B 3QP. Tel:
(0171) 636 5488. Fax: (0171) 636 4799.

OTHER USEFUL ADDRESSES

British Film Institute, £13.50 pa; concs available. 21 Stephen Street,
London W1M 1DJ. Tel: (0171) 255 1444.

British Guild of Travel Writers, £50 pa; professional association, open to
members whose income derives largely from travel reporting. 90
Corringway, London W8 3HA. Tel: (0181) 998 2223.

Theatre Writers' Union, the Administrator, c/o The Actors Centre, 1A
Tower Street, London WC2H 9ND. Tel: (0181) 673 6636.

Index